Biblical Criticism

BLOOMSBURY T&T CLARK GUIDES FOR THE PERPLEXED

Bloomsbury T&T Clark's Guides for the Perplexed are clear, concise and accessible introductions to thinkers, writers and subjects that students and readers can find especially challenging. Concentrating specifically on what it is that makes the subject difficult to grasp, these books explain and explore key themes and ideas, guiding the reader towards a thorough understanding of demanding material.

Guides for the Perplexed available from Bloomsbury T&T Clark:

New Testament and Jewish Law: A Guide for the Perplexed, James G. Crossley

The Origin of the Bible: A Guide for the Perplexed, Lee Martin McDonald

Paul: A Guide for the Perplexed, Timothy G. Gombis

A GUIDE FOR THE PERPLEXED

Biblical Criticism

ERYL W. DAVIES

B L O O M S B U R Y

LONDON · NEW DELHI · NEW YORK · SYDNEY

Bloomsbury T&T Clark

An imprint of Bloomsbury Publishing Plc

50 Bedford Square
London
WC1B 3DP
UK

175 Fifth Avenue
New York
NY 10010
USA

www.bloomsbury.com

First published 2013

British Library Cataloguing-in-Publication Data
A catalogue record for this book is available from the British Library.

ISBN: HB: 978-0-567-01306-4
PB: 978-0-567-14594-9

Library of Congress Cataloging-in-Publication Data
A catalog record for this book is available from the Library of Congress.

Typeset by Newgen Imaging Systems Pvt Ltd, Chennai, India
Printed and bound in Great Britain

CONTENTS

ABBREVIATIONS

BTB	*Biblical Theology Bulletin*
CBQ	*Catholic Biblical Quarterly*
NLH	*New Literary History*
JBL	*Journal of Biblical Literature*
JR	*Journal of Religion*
JSOT	*Journal for the Study of the Old Testament*
JSOTSup	*Journal for the Study of the Old Testament: Supplement Series*
JTS	*Journal of Theological Studies*
RIDA	*Revue Internationale des Droits de l'Antiquité*
SBL	*Society of Biblical Literature*
VT	*Vetus Testamentum*

PREFACE

Contemporary biblical scholarship has witnessed a variety of interpretative methods, and the aim of the present volume is to outline some of the fundamental principles which undergird certain of the more recent approaches to the interpretation of the Bible. Limitation of space has meant that only four of these approaches (reader-response criticism, feminist criticism, ideological criticism and postcolonial criticism) could be examined in any detail; however, the concluding chapter attempts to provide a briefer overview of three other approaches (rhetorical criticism, canonical criticism and ethical criticism) which seemed to me to deserve some attention. Other, no doubt equally significant, methods (such as structuralism, deconstruction and psycho-analytic criticism) have not been discussed, since their inclusion would have extended the present volume beyond what would have been practicable. A shorter version of Chapter One appeared under the title, 'Reader-response Criticism and Old Testament Studies', in R. Pope (ed.), *Honouring the Past and Shaping the Future: Religious and Biblical Studies in Wales,* and it appears here with the kind permission of its publishers, Gracewing.

I thank the staff at T & T Clark/Bloomsbury for their interest in the volume and for their help and guidance along the way. I am grateful to two of my colleagues in the School of Theology and Religious Studies at Bangor, Dr Lucy Huskinson and Dr David Tollerton, for their perceptive comments and criticisms which have helped to sharpen and clarify my position at many points. I am also grateful to my wife, Eirian, for her continued support and encouragement, and to my children, Manon, Llinos, Gethin and Osian, who, as always, provided some welcome diversion from the often arduous tasks of writing and research.

Eryl W. Davies
School of Theology and Religious Studies
Bangor University

INTRODUCTION

Our aim in this volume is to survey some of the major trends in contemporary discussions of the Bible, and to provide some indication of where biblical scholarship stands at present and the direction in which it seems to be going. The last four decades or so have witnessed a proliferation of new interpretative approaches and strategies – reader-response criticism, feminist criticism, ideological criticism and postcolonial criticism (to name but a few) – and traditional study of the Bible has had to accommodate new modes of inquiry and address questions that had previously been outside the purview of biblical scholars. Does a particular text have one meaning or many? What are the social, cultural, class, gender and racial issues at work in a particular passage? What kinds of influences are prompting the interpreter's perception of the Bible? These are the type of questions which the critical methods discussed in the present volume attempt to address.

But the application of these methods, in turn, raises a number of further questions that need to be considered. What are the principles and presuppositions that underlie each method? What are the distinctive characteristic features of each approach? What factors have contributed to the development of each mode of inquiry? What are the intellectual currents that have generated and guided each strategy? Exigencies of space have inevitably meant that only a small selection of current methods could be discussed in any detail; to have attempted to examine other approaches would have broadened the discussion well beyond what would have been manageable within the limits of the present volume. However, the concluding chapter provides a brief overview of a few other approaches in current biblical scholarship which seem to the present writer to be particularly significant and fruitful areas of scholarly inquiry.

The dominant approach in academic study of the Bible from the early nineteenth century until comparatively recently has been the historical-critical method.[1] This mode of inquiry emerged as part of the great intellectual revolution in sixteenth- and seventeenth-century Europe, and until the third quarter of the twentieth century it was regarded as the only method of biblical interpretation generally recognized as legitimate within the academy.[2] This approach tried to emulate the rigorous objectivity of the natural sciences, and it sought to engage in a study of the Bible uninfluenced by the interests and prejudices of the individual interpreter. Neutrality and objectivity were elevated as venerable virtues, and any hint of personal bias was regarded as an unhealthy intrusion into the discipline. The concern of the method – as its name implies – was basically historical, and its remit included deciphering the 'original' meaning of the text (by which was meant the meaning intended by the original author), determining the date and origins of the various biblical traditions, and examining the process by which they came into existence.

It is, perhaps, not surprising that in the postmodern world of crumbling certainties, many of the supposedly 'assured' results of the historical-critical approach have been radically questioned, if not completely overturned. There was a growing rebellion against the hegemony of the dominant paradigm, and its weaknesses and limitations were becoming increasingly apparent. Questions were raised concerning the dating of the sources behind the Pentateuch and, indeed, whether such 'sources' ever existed at all. Feminist biblical critics questioned the traditional self-image of historical criticism as an objective and disinterested scholarly pursuit, and argued that all interpreters came to the Bible with their own interests and presuppositions, which were bound to colour what they found in the text. Reader-response critics questioned the wisdom of trying to determine the meaning intended by the original author, for such information was no longer accessible and, in any case, all texts probably contained a surplus of meanings beyond what the original author intended to say. Moreover, the claim of the historical-critical approach to be the universally valid norm and the benchmark against which all other interpretations must be adjudicated, was similarly called into question, as scholars came to favour a plurality of exegetical methods and insisted that no single approach to the Bible could be regarded as definitive.

The emergence of new methods sweeping through the biblical landscape did not, however, involve the complete disappearance of the old. While it is true that a number of titles appeared triumphantly proclaiming the end of the historical-critical approach,[3] its demise did not indicate the clamorous closing down of an old epoch tentatively giving way to the tumultuous birth of a new one. As many adherents of the newer approaches readily conceded, it would have been mistaken to repudiate the historical-critical method altogether and reject the collective wisdom of previous generations of scholarly endeavour.[4] If historical-criticism was on the decline, it was not because of the force of the intellectual arguments against it, but simply because it no longer seemed appealing or exciting to a new generation of biblical scholars for whom other interests and concerns had assumed priority. While they recognized that the method would undoubtedly occupy an important place in biblical studies for the foreseeable future, there was a growing feeling that it had taken us about as far as we could go and that it was now time to pose new questions of the text and to open up the interpretative agenda of biblical scholarship to encompass broader areas of academic inquiry.

Coincidentally, the decline of the historical-critical method occurred at the same time as a resurgence of interest in modern literary criticism. Of course, the 'literary' approach to the Bible was by no means new, for the attempt of historical-critics to trace various sources behind the Pentateuch by separating earlier from later traditions was itself basically a 'literary' endeavour. However, the 1970s saw the emergence of new theoretical approaches applied to the Bible, and scholars became increasingly aware of the advantages that could accrue to the discipline of a close engagement with secular literary theory. The focus on the historical background and origin of the text was giving way to an emphasis on the internal operations of the text itself. Indeed, there was an enormous upsurge in the production of literary studies of the Bible, and *literary* methodologies were commonly applied to biblical narratives which had previously been analysed for their *historical* interest.[5] Adherents of these new approaches rejected as irrelevant the various hypotheses regarding the earlier stages underlying the present form of the text, for their focus was much more on appreciating the aesthetic qualities of the Bible in its present canonical form. Thus, for example, whereas classical source-critical analysis of the biblical material

regarded the presence of repetitions, inconsistencies or incoheren-
cies in the text as a clear sign of its composite nature, adherents
of the later literary approaches tended to regard such phenomena
as effective literary techniques deliberately deployed for a specific
purpose by the final redactors of the text.

By the 1980s, attention was beginning to turn away from the text
to the reader and the profound significance of the reading experience. The focus was no longer on the intention of the author or the
original context of the writing, but on the response of the reader
in determining the meaning and significance of the text. 'Meaning'
was no longer seen simply as the sole property of the text, and
the reader was no longer viewed merely as the one who performed
technical operations on the text (such as literary or lexical analysis)
in a fairly mechanical way. What the text contained was not 'meaning' as such, but a set of directions enabling the reader to assemble
a meaning, directions which each individual would carry out in his
or her own way. 'Meaning' was something that emerged from the
fruitful interaction between the text and its readers: the stimulus
of the text (its style and use of metaphors, etc.) was regarded as
interacting with the stimulus of readers (their background, values,
preconceptions, biases, etc.) in a way that made the text meaningful. The very act of reading was regarded as an active, constructive
exercise, for it was an activity that might alter our perception, stir
our emotion, and possibly spur us into action. By itself, the text
was just an inert object, a lifeless assemblage of paper, binding and
print. The role of the reader was to bring that text to life and, in
the words of Norman Holland, to play 'the part of the prince to the
sleeping beauty' (1975: 12).

Adherents of what came to be termed as the 'new' literary criticism of the Bible realized that if the biblical text was to be relevant
it had to resonate with the concerns of those who were reading it.
Indeed, one of the perceived weaknesses of the historical-critical
approach was that it had failed to relate in a meaningful way to
the society in which the work was done. There was a feeling that
biblical scholarship had become insular and introvert, and that
those engaged in a study of the Bible were expending their time
and energy trying to answer questions that nobody was asking.[6]
The Bible had become little more than an object of linguistic and
historical analysis, divorced from issues of contemporary concern,
and as a result there was a gap between the biblical 'experts' and

the layperson, between theological faculties and church members, between theory and praxis.

It was hardly surprising, therefore, that adherents of the newer methods reacted with some impatience to the way in which mainstream biblical scholarship had detached itself from the social and political issues of the day. For them, praxis was not an optional extra or a secondary, subsidiary enterprise, but a vital part of the interpretative process itself. They realized the importance of making their research *relevant*, for a scholarship that ignored the people would eventually be ignored *by* the people. Already in the 1960s, liberation theologians from Latin America had brought a new lease of life to the study of the Bible by ensuring that it addressed the needs of the people who were reading it. Their starting-point for theological reflection was not the biblical text, but the desperate situation of the poor and their cry for freedom from oppressive regimes. As Carlos Mesters observed in relation to the reading of the Bible by members of the base ecclesial communities in Brazil, the main hermeneutical task was not so much to interpret the Bible 'but to interpret life with the help of the Bible' (1989: 9). Biblical scholars from Africa and Asia were similarly aware of the social, political and economic struggles of the people for whom they were writing, and they realized that to make the Bible relevant was far more important than engaging in abstract theories about its formation and participating in philosophical debates about its content. The critical methods that they deployed emerged out of the specific hermeneutical and contextual needs of their audience and, far from being a remote, irrelevant exercise, the study of the Bible was a co-operate enterprise between the professionally trained scholar and the ordinary reader (see West 1993; 1999; West and Dube 1996).

The realization that biblical study must not remain a merely intellectual activity indulged in by comfortable academics was not lost on adherents of the newer methods of biblical criticism. Feminist biblical critics frequently approached the Bible from the perspective of women who had been marginalized by men and denied access to positions of authority and influence within the academy and within the church. The starting-point of postcolonial critics was the cruelty and injustice suffered by those who had been on the receiving end of oppressive colonial regimes. The recognition that study of the Bible was a dynamic activity and could be a powerful force for social change was to inaugurate a new and exciting era in critical study of the Bible.

The pursuit of rapidly changing fashions in biblical research, however, is not without its pitfalls and drawbacks. It must be admitted, for example, that much contemporary biblical criticism is difficult for the uninitiated to understand. The debates conducted by adherents of the new approaches are often so enmeshed in theoretical jargon and convoluted language that they may seem remote and even meaningless to the ordinary reader. New concepts – such as the 'implied author', the 'postulated reader' and the 'unreliable narrator' – have by now become part and parcel of the standard lexicon of biblical scholars, as have obscure technical terms such as 'deconstruction', 'synchronic' and 'diachronic', to name but a few. The use of such unfamiliar language often has the unfortunate effect of distancing the Bible from ordinary people, and entrenching the notion that its interpretation is the sole preserve of the academy and is something of interest only to a select group of 'insiders'. The situation is hardly helped by the tendency of adherents of these approaches to trot out exotic-sounding names of scholars whom they have read (or pretend to have read!) – scholars such as Jacques Derrida, Julia Kristeva, Roland Barthes and Louis Althusser – who have themselves created weird and esoteric coinages which few readers can be expected to understand. Indeed, ordinary readers who try to engage with some of the more recent methods may be forgiven for feeling as though they are overhearing a conversation conducted in a foreign language, and the more cynical among them may even harbour the suspicion that the use of such perplexing terminology by scholars arises out of a perverse desire to be deliberately obscure, or – worse still – is merely a ploy to lend a spurious authority to their pronouncements. Unless there is a degree of methodological clarity concerning the new strategies deployed by biblical scholars, lay people may well conclude that it is not worth the time or the effort to understand them properly and, as a result, biblical scholars will find themselves addressing the ever-increasing community of professional theologians and the seemingly shrinking community of ordinary readers. It is thus imperative that these methods reach a broader audience and be made interesting and stimulating to the non-specialist. After all, their purpose is to facilitate a new and fresh understanding of the biblical text, and if the methods remain obscure and perplexing there is a danger that, far from illuminating passages of Scripture, they may prove to be an impediment to understanding them.

It is important to recognize that the various critical methods discussed in this volume are by no means mutually exclusive; on the contrary, there is an easy rapprochement between them, and some share similar preoccupations and theoretical presuppositions. Many of the scholars discussed in the following chapters are engaged in a common interpretative vocation, whether this takes the form of resisting dominant interpretations of the Bible, or foregrounding the voice of the marginalized and excluded. Feminist biblical criticism and postcolonial criticism, for example, are united by a mutual resistance to any form of oppression – patriarchy in the case of the former, and colonialism in the case of the latter (see Kwok Pui-lan 2005). There is also a clear overlap between ideological criticism and reader-response criticism, and these methods have undoubtedly benefitted from engaging in dialogue with one another. But although the various 'biblical criticisms' discussed in this volume are often partners in a common cause, and although there are certain unifying aspects in their approach to the Bible, the distinction between them should not be blurred, for each has its own particular emphasis and each interprets the biblical text through its own particular angle of vision.

*　　*　　*

The most important question of all, however, has yet to be addressed, namely, what is the *point* of biblical criticism? Why bother with it in the first place? What difference will the application of the methods described in this volume make to our reading and understanding of the Bible? If these approaches have to be applied at all, why not confine them to undergraduate courses at universities rather than trouble ordinary, lay readers with the here-today, gone-tomorrow fads of the literary establishment? The fact is that ordinary readers – no doubt to the utter dismay of the professional biblical critic – are not particularly interested in textual puzzles that need to be resolved, or contradictions in the text that have to be reconciled, or ambiguities that have to be explained and clarified. Indeed, it could be argued that the kinds of theories advocated by contemporary biblical scholars only serve to spoil the simple, undiluted pleasure of reading and result in the loss of a direct and spontaneous response to the biblical text. Besides, if truth be told, are these new-fangled theories not just a fashionable exercise indulged in by academics with time on their hands, and discussed and analysed by them to the point of tedium merely because they are regarded as providing a valuable passport to academic and intellectual respectability?

While one can readily sympathize with such scepticism, and while it is true that anyone can read the Bible without the benefit of any of the methods discussed in the following chapters, the fact is that applying biblical criticism to particular passages can prove helpful and illuminating, whether the reader be the lay person consulting the Bible for their own personal devotion, or a pastor preparing a sermon or address, or a trained biblical scholar engaged in detailed exegesis of the text. The potential rewards of familiarizing ourselves with contemporary biblical practices are many, and it may be helpful at the outset to suggest three ways in which our reading of the Bible may be enriched – and perhaps altered – as a result of recent scholarly approaches.

In the first place, applying these methods allows us to read the Bible from a different perspective, and may prove a useful corrective to the often unguarded assumption that our own (white? middle-class? male?) understanding of the text is the most natural and obvious reading. Indeed, writing this volume has itself been a learning experience for the present writer, for the process of discussing, explaining and analysing the various theories has encouraged me to view the Bible from perspectives other than my own. Reading David Clines' *Interested Parties,* for example, opened my eyes for the first time to the ideological overtones entrenched in the Bible and in its interpretation; reading the works of feminist biblical scholars, such as Phyllis Trible and Elisabeth Schüssler Firoenza, increased my awareness of the gender bias inherent in the biblical material and the way in which male commentators have interpreted the biblical text in a way that consolidates and reinforces patriarchal values; reading the lucidly written volumes by R. S. Sugaritharajah brought home to me a heightened awareness of the Eurocentric bias and racial nuances present in familiar interpretations of the biblical text, and encouraged me to consider how the Bible might be viewed by ethnic minorities or by people who have been subject to the oppression of colonial rule.

Secondly, applying the critical methods described in this volume may serve as a potent reminder that reading the Bible is not the harmless pursuit that we often suppose it to be, for biblical texts can be summoned in support of various causes, not all of which, by any means, are for the common good. The danger of appealing to the Bible in a simplistic, uncritical way may be seen in the use made of it by those who freely quote biblical texts to vilify gays and lesbians or to legitimate racist domination and exploitation. The fact is that selective and discriminatory use of the Bible has proved oppressive for Jews, heretics, women, slaves and people of colour, to name but a few in the ever-increasing roll-call of persecuted minorities. Adherents of some of the recent scholarly approaches are only too aware that the Bible can function not only as a holy text but as a 'savage' text when it is used to victimize and marginalize people on account of their race, colour, gender or sexual orientation.[7] Feminist critics have shown how the Bible has been deployed as a weapon to keep women in their place and to exclude them from positions of authority and leadership in the church (Chapter Two). Postcolonial critics have demonstrated how supporters of colonialism used narratives from the Old Testament as a model and justification for the subjugation of the native inhabitants of the colonized countries (Chapter Four). Far too often in the past an eclectic selection of texts has been cited in order to uphold a particular moral position, resulting in highly prejudicial views – whether concerning anti-Semitism, sexual proclivity, gender equality, economic status or whatever – being justified on biblical grounds. Familiarity with some of the strategies outlined in this volume may thus serve as a warning against the danger of bolstering a particular position by an apologetic assemblage of proof-texts, a procedure still commonly used today, but one that can only bring the entire Bible into disrepute.

Thirdly, application of recent scholarly approaches should alert us to the fact that the act of reading the Bible is not the simple, straightforward exercise we might think. The Bible is a multifaceted work that speaks in a range of voices on a variety of issues. It is neither a coherent nor a unified book, but is riddled with contradictions and ambiguities, and consequently it often emits conflicting signals. Reading what we may imagine to be the plain, obvious, natural meaning of Scripture overlooks the fact that different people may derive different – and perhaps mutually exclusive – principles from the same text, depending, as often as not, on the message they want to extract from the pages of Scripture. Familiarity with the principles underlying reader-response criticism (Chapter One) and ideological criticism (Chapter Three) may help to bring a heightened awareness of our own working assumptions and predispositions as we read the Bible. How has our professional commitments or religious allegiances affected our understanding of a particular text? How has our geographical location and cultural context contributed to our perception of a particular passage? How has our ethnic identity or our allegiance to a particular political ideology influenced our interpretation? How has our theological or confessional stance (or lack thereof) predetermined what we will find in the text? As the chapter on 'ideological criticism' will hopefully demonstrate, awareness of our own presuppositions and prejudices is the first step towards entering into a meaningful dialogue with others.

*   *   *

A book on 'biblical criticism' inevitably entails discussion of both Testaments and this has meant tentatively moving from the safe haven of my own specialist training in the Old Testament to focus on some issues relating to the New. Although examples will be taken from a variety of texts throughout the biblical corpus, the reader will no doubt detect a distinct bias towards texts from the Hebrew Bible. No doubt some will want to challenge the choice of methods discussed and will bemoan the fact that other, equally significant, methods – such as structuralism, deconstruction, psycho-analytic criticism, queer criticism, etc. – have been ignored; but the inclusion of these would have considerably enlarged the present volume. Indeed, the fact that students of the Bible are now confronted with such a bewildering variety of methods and theoretical practices is surely something to be welcomed, for it indicates that biblical studies is not a sterile, moribund discipline but an area of study that is always open to new challenges and to new developments in the field. These developments have radically changed the ways we think about texts, and this means that the twenty-first century is an exciting and productive time for the study of the Bible. If the present volume manages to convey some of that excitement, it will have more than served its purpose.

CHAPTER ONE

Reader-response criticism

If we could have interviewed Shakespeare he probably would have expressed his intentions in writing *Hamlet* in a way which we should find most unsatisfactory. We would still quite rightly insist on finding meanings in *Hamlet* . . . which were probably far from clearly formulated in Shakespeare's conscious mind.

R. Wellek and A. Warren

The study of a literary work should concern not only the actual text but also, and in equal measure, the actions involved in responding to that text.

Wolfgang Iser

For most Biblical scholars reader-response criticism is worn like an overcoat: it is an engaging and currently fashionable garment to wear in public, but it can be shed when the weather changes.

S. E. Porter

Traditionally, the interest of biblical scholars has focused on questions of historical import. Working within the constraints of the historical-critical method, their aim was to analyse the biblical texts as objectively as possible in order to reconstruct the historical events to which they referred. The first step was usually to place the biblical text in its historical context and to raise questions concerning its authorship, date, place of writing and social setting. Once such questions were answered, the text of the Bible could be viewed as a window through which the biblical scholar could glimpse historical reality.

In recent years, however, some scholars have expressed dissatisfaction with such a one-sided, historical approach to the Bible and have argued that it is time for the interest of the scholarly community to move away from the moment of the text's production to the moment of its reception. Instead of focusing on the text's author and the complicated issue of authorial intent, biblical scholars should concern themselves with the text's reader, and the role of the reader in the production of meaning. In this regard, developments in secular literary theory, notably reader-response criticism, are viewed as helpful in suggesting the direction in which biblical interpretation should proceed. The aim of the present chapter is to trace the rise of the reader-response movement in literary criticism, to examine its impact on the study of the Bible, and to demonstrate how the application of reader-response criticism might illuminate our reading of the gospel of Mark.

Reader-response criticism in literary theory

In literary theory, the phenomenon known as 'reader-response criticism' emerged as a reaction to the views of the so-called American New Critics who flourished in the 1940s and 1950s. The New Critics had emphasized that each literary work was to be regarded as an autonomous, self-sufficient entity, which was to be studied in its own terms, without reference to its cultural and historical context and without regard to the intention of its author or the response of its reader. Meaning was something that inhered exclusively in the text itself, and any extraneous factors were to be discounted, for they would only lead the interpreter astray. The duty of the reader was to come as close as possible to the meaning embedded in the text. Thus, knowledge of the text's production, or of the author's purpose in writing, even if such data could be recovered, were irrelevant, for once the literary work had been composed it led a life completely independent of its author. The matter was stated very succinctly by Wimsatt and Beardsley in their seminal essay, 'The Intentional Fallacy', which is sometimes regarded as the New Critics' manifesto: 'The poem is not the critic's own and not the author's (it is detached from the author at birth and goes about the world beyond his power . . . to control it)' (1946: 70). It was thus a 'fallacy' to believe that the meaning of a literary composition should correspond to the author's intention; on the contrary, once the author had written his text, the umbilical cord had been broken and he or she no longer had any control over how it was to be interpreted. The author became, in effect, just another reader, and could claim no special prerogative of understanding a literary work by virtue of his having composed it. Any attempt to determine the author's aims and purpose in writing was merely a distraction, for the text was considered to be a free-standing and self-sustaining entity which was regarded as the repository of its own meaning. Every interpretation of a text must therefore find its authentication in the text itself, and not in any extrinsic factors that might be thought to lie behind it.

By abstracting the text from its author and isolating it from its cultural and historical context, the New Critics were able to focus their attention entirely on the literary composition itself. The result of such an approach was inevitably an increased attention to the 'words on the page' and a call for a scrupulously 'close' reading of the text, for only thus could the literary work be broached in a neutral fashion and an attempt be made to determine its definitive meaning. 'Objectivity' was the keynote of the New Critical enterprise, and it was emphasized that there was no place in literary interpretation for subjective impressions or personal intuitions. Only when such intuitive factors had firmly been set to one side could the critic properly begin to analyse the content and structure of the literary text and examine the rich complexity of its meaning. That meaning was regarded as timeless, unchanging and universal; what the text means now is what it had always meant, and the task that faced its readers was to discover, to the best of their ability, what that meaning was.

The text-centred approach of the New Critics, however, gradually came to be viewed as grossly inadequate, for there was an increasing awareness that literary compositions could not be hermetically sealed from history and isolated from the cultural context in which they were written. Nor, indeed, could they be studied in isolation from their readers. The role of the reader could not simply be marginalized or ignored, for readers were active participants in the determination of literary meaning and creative contributors to the interpretative process. Literary compositions should not be prised away from their contexts of meaning and response, for texts meant what they meant to particular people at particular times and in particular circumstances. The subject (reader) and the object (text) were indivisibly bound together, and the relationship between them was a dynamic process, for texts only became alive and meaningful when people became involved with them and responded to them.

This new approach, known as 'reader-response criticism', clearly represented a radical departure from the type of methodology advocated by the New Critics.[1] While the latter had exalted the text over both author and reader, the reader-response critics sought to challenge the privileged status of the text and emphasize instead the role of the reader and the profound significance of the reading experience. While the New Critics had dismissed the reader's response as subjective and hopelessly relativistic, the reader-response critics argued that the interplay between text and reader was of considerable significance for the interpretation of a literary work.

This interplay was particularly emphasized by Wolfgang Iser, who was one of the leading advocates of the reader-response approach (1974; 1978). As the quotation at the beginning of this chapter indicates, Iser argued that the reader must take into account not only the text itself but also the actions involved in responding to that text. Such actions were determined, in large measure, by the literary text itself, for the text was usually full of gaps and indeterminacies, and it was precisely these gaps that activated readers' faculties and stimulated their creative participation. The reader was invited to engage with the text by filling in the blanks and inferring that which the text had withheld. Reading was a process of anticipation and retrospection which involved the deciphering of words and sentences, the relating of parts to the whole, the modifying of perspectives, the revising of assumptions, the readjustment of perceptions, the asking of questions and the supplying of answers. Instead of looking *behind* the text for the meaning, the meaning was to be found *in front of* the text, in the active participation of the reader (Iser 1980: 106–19).

In a similar vein, the American critic, Stanley Fish, another leading figure in the reader-response movement, argued that the object of critical attention should be the experience of the reader, rather than any objective structures or patterns in the text itself. Far from playing a passive, submissive role, readers were active agents in the making of meaning and were encouraged to reflect upon the impact that the literary work had had upon them. The literary text was not so much an object to be analysed as an effect to be experienced. Consequently, the fundamental question that should be asked of any text was not, 'What does it mean?' but 'What does it *do*?' and the task of the critic was to analyse *'the developing responses of the reader in relation to words as they succeeded one another in time'* (1972: 387–8; his italics). Understood in this way, the act of reading involved far more than a perception of what was written; it was rather to be regarded as a dynamic process, an activity, an 'event'.

One of the effects of such an approach, of course, was to undermine all belief in the objectivity of the autonomous text, and emphasis came to be placed instead on the indeterminacy of the text's meaning. Since the reader was called upon to co-operate with the text in the production of meaning, and since each text would be actualized by different readers in different ways, allowance had to be made for a broad spectrum of possible readings of the same text. The view cherished by the New Critics that a text contained a single, definitive, authoritative meaning, accessible to all and sundry and wholly resistant to historical change, was abandoned, and texts were made to speak what the reader of the moment wanted them to say. Of course, the reader-response critics were only too aware that, once the burden of meaning was placed upon the reader, the door would inevitably be flung open to a plurality of divergent – and perhaps even conflicting – interpretations. But this was not generally regarded as a problem; on the contrary, the vast range of possible interpretations merely testified to the text's richness and inexhaustibility. Indeed, this was what made literary texts worthy of the name. Literature thrived on subjective perceptions, and the more interpretations it attracted, the more profound the text appeared to be. Consequently, different readings of literary texts were not merely tolerated but positively encouraged; rival voices were not simply permitted but actively cultivated. The reader-response critics were thus happy to promote the idea that texts were capable of producing an infinite variety of diverse readings and they saw no need to adjudicate between them, for all readings had equal validity and could be regarded as equally legitimate. There was thus no need to be in the least embarrassed by differing interpretations of the same text; on the contrary, they were to be welcomed, for the response of the reader to the text was at least as interesting, if not more so, than the content of the text itself.

Some critics, however, were aware that the phenomenon of reader-response criticism was not without its attendant dangers, and that investing so much authority in the reader could have its potential drawbacks. The main concern was that the strategy might result in a seemingly uncontrollable proliferation of subjective and idiosyncratic readings, and that readers might abuse their new-found authority by arbitrarily imposing their own meaning on the text and riding rough-shod over the aims and intentions of the original author. Surely, it was argued, authors had *some* moral right to be understood as they had intended? Surely the significance of a text for a reader should not be completely at variance with its significance for its author? One of the most able advocates of this view was the American scholar, E. D. Hirsch. According to Hirsch, to deny the privileged status of the author as the determiner of the text's meaning was to reject the only compelling normative principle that could lend validity to an interpretation, for without the concept of authorial intent there was no adequate criterion to adjudicate between competing notions of textual meaning.[2] Hirsch's concern in this regard was clearly to avoid the vagaries of subjectivism, for he believed that, without the concept of 'authorial intent' interpretation would simply degenerate into a chaotic free-for-all in which every reading of a text was as valid as any other and in which readers could find in a text whatever they went there to look for. Such a state of affairs was clearly intolerable in Hirsch's view, and was merely a recipe for interpretative anarchy.

Like the New Critics, Hirsch believed that the author's 'intention' had been objectified in the text, and that each text therefore had a single, determinate meaning. There was thus only one correct interpretation of any given text, and it was the task of the interpreter to recover it. Of course, this did not mean that different interpreters could not find some new *significance* in a text; clearly they could, but discovering the text's 'significance' was not necessarily the same as discovering the text's 'meaning'. The text's 'meaning' was essentially what it meant for the original author, while the text's 'significance' was what it meant for subsequent readers.[3] The latter, according to Hirsch, was susceptible to change; the former, on the other hand, was complete and final, immutable and fixed for all time (1967: 255). Consequently, Hirsch argued that it was the interpreter's duty to respect the author's intention, and unless there was '*a powerful overriding value in disregarding an author's intention . . . we who interpret as a vocation should not disregard it*' (1976: 90; his italics). Even if the intentions of the original authors were not accessible (since they may be dead or have forgotten what their intended meaning was), the interpreter had an ethical responsibility to reconstruct the *probable* authorial intent. Just as in everyday situations the intention of the speaker was considered an important determinant of the meaning of his words, so the intention of the author of a literary work should be regarded as the final arbiter of the text's meaning. So convinced was Hirsch that there must be some congruence between the meaning intended by the author and the significance construed by the reader that he posed the following questions to those critics who cavalierly dismissed the notion of authorial meaning:

> When you write a piece of criticism, do you want me to disregard *your* intention and original meaning? Why do you say to me 'That is not what I meant at all; that is not it at all?' Why do you ask me to honor the ethics of language for your writings when you do not honor them for the writings of others? (1976: 91)

Hirsch continued:

> Few critics fail to show moral indignation when their meaning is distorted in reviews and other interpretations of their interpretations. But their sensitivity is often one-way, and in this they show an inconsistency amounting to a double standard – one for their authors, another for themselves (1976: 91).

One of the problems with Hirsch's argument, however, was that the critics whom he was addressing were presumably alive and well and able to respond indignantly to any misinterpretation or misrepresentation of their words; but in the case of authors who were long dead there was no one to chastise readers for going down the wrong path, and consequently they could never be certain whether they had correctly understood the author's meaning. To speak of 'authorial intent' merely brought literary critics to an inaccessible hypothetical realm, which they had no means of reconstructing with any confidence.[4] The process of recovering authorial intent required the critic to enter into what Hirsch called 'the author's mental and experiential world' and this increasingly came to be seen as an unrealizable ideal. Nor was the critic's task made any easier if, perchance, authors had thoughtfully provided their readers with explicit evidence of their intentions, for it by no means followed that they had provided a reliable commentary upon their own work.[5] Writers were not always in full possession of their own meaning, and they were as liable to errors and misinterpretations of their own work almost as much as any other reader.[6] Moreover, authors sometimes failed to frame their message correctly and to express precisely what they meant, and in such cases the critic was better placed than the authors themselves to elucidate the meaning of what had been written.

This meant, of course, that the meaning of a work was by no means exhausted by its author's intentions, and that texts may have layers of meaning of which their authors were unaware and which they did not intend or foresee. Once the text had been released by its author it may reach an audience for whom it was not originally intended and may generate readings that differ from those that the author had in mind as the work had been composed. Consequently, Hirsch's argument that any given text had a single determinate meaning came to be regarded as naïve and misguided, for texts by their very nature lent themselves to be read in different ways and were far too rich and multifaceted to be exhausted by a single interpretation. Indeed, if literary texts were worthy of the name, they ought to be able to accommodate a number of different meanings. Hirsch's distinction between a text's 'meaning' (identified with the author's intention) and its 'significance' (i.e. its meaning-to-the-reader) was regarded as disingenuous, and it was argued that it was doubtful whether any literary text would (or was even intended to) convey one and the same meaning to every reader.[7] But even if Hirsch's distinction was allowed to stand, and that 'meaning' was equated with authorial intention, it was most unlikely that any two readers would agree as to what exactly that intention *was*. The reason for such disagreement was that the 'intention' discerned by the interpreter was itself the product of interpretation, and consequently there was more than a whiff of suspicion that the process advocated by Hirsch could only result in a vicious circle: the supposed intention reconstructed by interpreters was then being used by them in support of the meaning which they claimed to have discovered in the text.

The main problem with Hirsch's argument, therefore, was that authorial meaning was not as stable or determinate as he would have liked to suppose. Claims to know what the author must have intended, or even how a particular text would have been understood by the original audience, were regarded as extremely speculative and unproven. Moreover, Hirsch's argument forced the literary critic to enter the unfamiliar realm of psychological analysis, for if one were to speak of 'authorial meaning' it became necessary to clarify what the meaning of 'meaning' was in such a context. If meaning was confined to that which passed through the reflective conscience of the author, was not the critic ignoring the fact that at least part of a text's meaning may derive from the author's subconscious? Thus when literary critics referred blandly to 'authorial intention' did they have in mind the author's conscious or unconscious intention, and in any case, were they in any position to distinguish between them? The problem of discerning authorial intent, or even probable authorial intent, came to be regarded as so difficult and complex that most literary critics began to wonder why they should bother to undertake such an intrinsically impossible task.

But having decided that the issue of authorial intent was deeply problematic and could not provide the basis for judging the validity of a given interpretation, literary critics were faced with a problem that seemed equally intractable, namely, that of deciding whether a particular interpretation represented a true understanding of a text or a distorted one. For if the author's role as the supreme arbiter of the text's meaning was to be discounted, what could possibly take its place? What other criteria could be used to decide whether a particular interpretation was satisfactory? How was the literary critic to distinguish between a proper response to a text and an improper one? Without some validation of meaning and significance, there seemed nothing to prevent readers from indulging in the most fanciful, tendentious and idiosyncratic interpretations; without some safeguards and constraints, there was nothing to prevent them from imputing to a text a meaning or significance which it clearly could not bear. Of course, some of the dyed-in-the-wool reader-response critics responded to such concerns with gay abandon, claiming that there was no such thing as an 'improper' response to a text, and that each reader should be his or her own judge as to what the meaning of any text might be. But some felt decidedly uneasy at the thought of such excessive interpretative freedom, and they were only too conscious of the problems that might ensue if interpreters were allowed to exercise such sovereignty over the text. Surely, it was argued, there must be certain limits to the way readers could legitimately interpret a text, otherwise it would be virtually impossible for literary interpreters to conduct a rational and meaningful debate. Interpretative pluralism was fine in theory, but if that led to the ineluctable conclusion that any interpretation was as good as any other, and that all readings were equally valid, was not some constraint needed upon the interpreter's freedom? Although there was no desire to return to the view of the New Critics that a text could be reduced to a single, determinate meaning, it was felt that the sheer variability of peoples' responses to texts could prove problematic. Was there some way in which the multiplicity of possible meanings could be narrowed down? Was it possible to argue in favour of a 'limited pluralism', or was this simply a contradiction in terms? There must surely be some way to exclude interpretations that were inherently improbable and to dismiss readings that were clearly perversions and distortions of the text's meaning. The question was, however, who decides? Whose reading counts? Who had the competence and authority to validate a given interpretation? The answer to this imponderable was provided by Stanley Fish.

The interpretative community

Fish recognized that reader-response critics would not want to embrace a theory in which a literary text had a single, correct, definitive meaning (since that would violate its very essence as literature), but nor would they want to embrace a theory in which a literary text could receive as many readings as there were readers (since that would effectively preclude rational inquiry and principled debate). Literary texts should be open to a number of different readings but not necessarily to any reading or all readings. What was required was a theory that would accommodate a diversity of interpretations and yet was sufficiently constrained to prevent those interpretations from being completely arbitrary (Fish 1989: 70–1). It was to meet this need that Fish evolved his theory of the 'interpretive community'.[8]

Interpretation, according to Fish, always takes place within a specific context and the interpreter functions within the norms, standards and goals appropriate to that context. Individual interpreters were therefore, paradoxically, both free and constrained, for they were perfectly at liberty to proffer their own interpretation of a text, but knew that the interpretative community of which they were part would provide the necessary checks against unbridled subjectivity and would simply renounce interpretations that were completely whimsical or fanciful. Interpreters were therefore only too aware that idiosyncratic interpretations would be self-defeating, for they knew that their efforts at interpretation would have failed if no one else had been persuaded by their reading. The interpretative community thus functioned as a kind of censor, accepting some readings as normative, and rejecting others as untenable, and in this way a critical consensus was established. Fish's theory also managed to account for the relative stability and predictability of readers' responses to a text, for interpreters were constrained in their interpretation by the beliefs and practices of the community of readers to which they belonged. Members of each community held certain interpretative strategies in common, and it was these strategies that helped to shape, guide and direct a particular interpretation and to provide the necessary criteria for judging its validity. If different readers responded to the same text in different ways it was because they belonged to different interpretative communities; alternatively, if the same reader responded to a given text in different ways it was because he or she belonged to more than one interpretative community. The importance of Fish's theory was that it involved a relocation of interpretative authority from the text or its author to the community of readers to which the interpreter belonged. Interpreters were abundantly aware of their responsibility to the corporate enterprise of interpretation, and they knew that there was a mechanism firmly in place to ensure that individual fancy would eventually give way to general acceptance.

Although the emphasis on the role of the reader in secular literary criticism was something of a gradual and tranquil revolution, it nevertheless represented a significant shift in perspective. The authority of the text, which had been such a central tenet for the New Critics, had now been supplanted by the authority of its readers, who had installed themselves in a position of power.

The reader-response critics had managed to challenge the privileged status of the text, displace it from its position, centre-stage, and substitute the reader in its place. For some literary critics, this shift proved to be a liberating experience, for the tyranny of the text was replaced by the freedom of the individual reader, who now became the sole arbiter of the text's meaning; for others, it proved to be a retrograde step, since it doomed the text to a veritable kaleidoscope of unstable interpretations. But the change in emphasis brought with it a heightened awareness of precisely what was involved in the act of reading, and it had the salutary effect of making the reader more self-conscious of his or her own response to the text. Readers began to realize that it was not enough to ask, simply, 'What does the text say?'; rather, they were encouraged to pose more pertinent and penetrating questions, such as, 'What does the text say to *me*?' and (even more importantly), 'What do *I* say to *it*?' (Jauss 1982: 146–7). The text, in effect, opened itself up to a kind of dialogue between two interlocutors, and the reader was challenged to contribute with questions and reactions and to engage in a meaningful dialogue with the text.

Reader-response criticism and the Bible

It has become something of cliché to claim that developments in biblical studies lag behind those in secular literary criticism by some 20 or 30 years, but it is nevertheless a cliché that contains an element of truth. While literary critics in the 1930s and 1940s were declaring authorial intent to be irrelevant, biblical scholars even in the 1960s and 1970s were still operating, for the most part, within the author-centred method of interpretation.[9] The types of questions usually addressed to a biblical book (as even a cursory glance at the standard 'Introductions' to the Old and New Testaments will testify) were: When and where did the biblical authors live? What sources did they have at their disposal? What could be known about their background and the circumstances in which they wrote? Historical questions of this kind were commonly regarded as a necessary prelude before the more fundamental question could be tackled, namely, 'What did the author mean?' The concept of authorial meaning was important, for the underlying assumption of biblical scholars (seldom expressly articulated and seldom seriously questioned) was that the biblical author had intended to communicate a specific message to a specific audience, and that it was the goal of the interpreter to discover what that meaning was. The meaning of the message was not necessarily what it had been taken to mean by the church or synagogue over the centuries, but what it had meant to the original author who had composed it.

That such interest should have been evinced by biblical scholars in the intention of the original author was, perhaps, not altogether surprising, given that most had been trained in the time-honoured discipline of historical criticism. One of the aims of this discipline in its various manifestations (source-criticism, form-criticism, redaction-criticism) was to illuminate what the author of the text might have meant. Source-criticism's contribution to this aim was to enable biblical scholars to trace the various compositional stages behind the text, thus allowing them to focus upon the original words of the author, as opposed to their later editorial accretions; form-criticism's contribution was to investigate the literary conventions with which the authors may have been familiar and which may have helped them to fashion their message; redaction-criticism's contribution was to enable the biblical exegete to discern the intentions of the authors and the overarching theological purpose of their composition by examining the way in which they had assembled the various fragments of tradition into a unified whole. Although each of these methodologies involved a detailed analysis of the text, they were all geared to answering the question: 'What did the text mean to its author?'[10] Once this question had been answered, and the authorial meaning had been discovered, biblical exegetes were regarded as having achieved their goal.

During the 1960s and 1970s, however, some scholars expressed certain misgivings about such an author-centred approach, although their disquiet was occasioned not so much by their conviction that biblical scholars were asking the wrong questions, as by a growing realization that the questions being asked were almost impossible to answer. If, as was generally agreed, most of the writings of the Bible were either anonymous or pseudonymous, how could biblical scholars even begin to contemplate the quest for authorial meaning? How could they possibly discern what the original author meant if they did not even know who the original author was? Moreover, the quest for authorial intent was complicated by the fact that many of the books of the Old Testament were composite creations which had been revised over a period of several centuries by succeeding generations of editors; consequently, it was felt that even to speak of an 'original author', as though the books in question were the product of a single, creative mind, was misguided. But perhaps the strongest opposition to the traditional approach came from those who were concerned with the issue of hermeneutics, for it was argued that to confine the significance of the text to the intention of the original author courted the risk of shutting up the meaning of the Bible in the past and turning it into an artefact of purely antiquarian interest, of little relevance for contemporary Western culture.

Given such misgivings, it was perhaps inevitable that the attention of biblical scholars should begin to turn to the text itself rather than the author who had composed it. Studies emerged which subjected the text to close, critical scrutiny by examining the themes, images, style and structure of a particular passage or book, and it was felt that the best way to broach the text was to understand it in its own terms, unencumbered by any concern for the original author's 'intention'. Of course, scholars who advocated this approach were not always in complete agreement as to what form of the biblical text should be the object of study. According to some, biblical interpreters should concern themselves with the meaning of the 'original' text (in so far as it could be reconstructed), while others argued that it was the text in its final form, complete with editorial modifications, that should be the focus of scholarly analysis. But whichever form of the text was considered to be the most appropriate object of study, such an interest in the text itself, regardless of the circumstances of its composition, brought biblical scholars in the 1970s to adopt an approach akin to that of the New Critics of the 1940s and 1950s.

Some scholars, however, expressed their reservations about adopting such an exclusively text-centred approach to the Bible. The weakness of such a strategy was that it left the reader out of account. The biblical text had been regarded as so self-sufficient that there had been little, if any, analysis of the reading experience; indeed, the act of reading had been regarded as such an obvious and commonplace activity that there had seemed nothing particularly interesting or significant to say about it. In so far as the reader had been considered at all, he or she had been regarded as merely the disposable extractor of textual meaning (Fish 1980: 158). So pervasive had been the influence of the historical-critical method among biblical scholars that the role of the reader had been either completely ignored or, at best, dispatched to the sidelines.

It was not until the 1980s that biblical scholars began seriously to examine how texts affected their readers. Influenced by developments in secular literary criticism, it was argued that readers of the Bible had occupied a subordinate position for far too long, and that it was time that they were elevated to their rightful position and accorded a place of importance in the interpretative process. Traditional interest in the text's production needed to be supplemented, if not replaced, by an interest in the text's reception. Of course, it was realized that this would involve a radical reorientation of scholarly approaches to the Bible, and that, to some extent, the very ground-plan of the discipline would have to be redrawn. The time had come for the historical-critical approach to the text, which had reigned supreme for almost two centuries, to give way to a more literary, non-historical approach. Advocates of such a change were careful not to deny the enduring significance of the historical-critical method, for it had undoubtedly proved productive in the past and had yielded valuable results. But it was felt that such an approach did not always do full justice to the biblical texts themselves. When historical questions were put to the texts, they would return the appropriate historical answers; but historical questions did not constitute the only legitimate means of access to the Bible, for the text could just as well be considered as a literary document. This was not to beat a retreat from the rigours of historical investigation; it was merely to recognize that there were limits to the information that could be gleaned about the biblical authors, their sources and the circumstances in which they wrote.

It was, of course, realized that the transition from the historical-critical to the literary-critical approach was not one that many biblical scholars would find particularly easy or congenial, for it involved a different critical orientation to that with which they had hitherto been accustomed. The interests of literary theorists seemed alien to the traditional interests of biblical scholars, and it was readily conceded that many would probably balk at the importation of a methodology that seemed so new and unfamiliar. Yet, such a dramatic shift in perspective seemed to many the best hope for the future of the discipline. There were interpretative problems for which the methodologies traditionally deployed no longer seemed appropriate and where the application of insights from contemporary literary criticism could yield more satisfying results.

The above outline of developments in scholarly approaches to the Bible is no doubt overly general and there are certainly many twists and turns in the debate that cannot be documented here, due to exigencies of space. But the broad outline provided does suggest that in biblical studies, as in secular literary criticism, attention has been focused at different times on the author, the text and the reader.[11] Perhaps the only surprising factor, in retrospect, is that the role of the reader should have been neglected for so long by biblical scholars, for without the reader there would be no point to the text and no purpose to the act of writing. By now, the importance of reader-response criticism is widely recognized in mainstream biblical scholarship. The new approach has spawned readings of the biblical text from a variety of different perspectives (feminist, ecological, black, liberation, etc.), though many biblical scholars are still more inclined to advocate a close reading of the text than a detailed analysis of the reading process. Some continue to align themselves with the historical-critical approach and cling tenaciously to the tried and tested methods of biblical interpretation. For them, the new emphasis on the reader is regarded as damaging to the received notions of the aims of biblical criticism and it is seen as playing havoc with traditional ideas of authorial and textual authority. There is much evidence to suggest, however, that an increasing number of scholars are, in principle, open to the new methodology,[12] although many are understandably wary, lest the discipline should enter a minefield from which it may find it difficult to extricate itself.

One concern, frequently expressed, is that once the reader is brought into play problems will occur which would simply not arise if interest were confined to the text. At least the traditional approach, for all its perceived faults, had the merit of precision and clarity and did not have to concern itself with the idiosyncrasies of the individual reader; the reader-response approach, on the other hand, seems nebulous by comparison, and difficult to define and analyse. The act of reading seems so intangible and elusive that biblical scholars who attempt to analyse it are in danger of being drawn into the realm of psychology, which is outside the province of their expertise. But the main problem with the new approach was the promiscuous instability of textual meaning to which it might give rise and the vagaries of interpretation which it might generate. In this regard, the concerns expressed by biblical scholars were similar to those voiced by many of the New Critics when reader-response criticism threatened to encroach upon their domain. Would not the door be opened to a veritable flood of impressionistic and idiosyncratic interpretations? Would not the strategy provide a license for each reader to interpret the text as he or she liked? Would not objective scholarship give way to an aberrant subjectivity? Would a multiplicity of readings not bring the entire discipline into disrepute? It is in this regard that Fish's concept of the 'interpretive community' may prove suggestive for biblical interpretation.

Readers of the Bible are usually associated with two distinct interpretative communities. Many will be members of the church or synagogue, and these institutions will provide them with certain conventions and instructions as to how the biblical text should be correctly interpreted. Others will be members of the academic community, and will pursue their study of Scripture in the context of a secular institution, which will have its own guidelines and strategies as to how biblical interpretation should proceed. Of course, to compartmentalize readers of the Bible in this way is perhaps overly simplistic, for there will be some readers who will belong to neither community and others who will belong to both (perhaps by virtue of pursuing their academic study of the Bible within church-based institutional structures). Moreover, within these larger interpretative communities there will be other, smaller communities, each with its own legacy to uphold, its own tradition to preserve, and its own vested interests to promote. But whatever its size and nature, readers of the Bible will always be situated in *some* context (for interpretation never occurs in a vacuum) and that context will usually determine the perspective from which they will proceed. Those who read the Bible cannot but be influenced by the community that taught them *how* to read it, and they will be conditioned to look at a text from a particular angle, informed by the interpretative disposition of the community of which they are part. If it is the goal of a particular interpretative community to read the Bible in a certain way, the text will be viewed with eyes already informed by the aims, beliefs and presuppositions of the interpretative community in question. Thus, for example, liberation theologians will understand the Bible against the background of a specific agenda in whose direction the Bible will be made to point. Likewise, feminist scholars will be predisposed to interpret the Bible in ways that uphold the feminist cause.[13] Often, members of such interpretative communities will have little confidence in studies produced by 'outsiders', for their firm conviction is that only those who have shared the particular experiences and concerns of the group can properly speak on its behalf.

The fact that there exist various interpretative communities means that the biblical text will inevitably be broached from a variety of different perspectives. Yet, biblical interpretation is not thereby doomed to descend into interpretative anarchy, for each community will have certain interpretative strategies that will delimit the ways in which a text can be read, discussed and critiqued.[14] The community will determine the range of meanings a given text can accommodate, and will adjudicate between readings that are admissible and those that are misguided. Each interpretative community will have its own criteria of evidence and its own measures of adequacy, and any given interpretation will be deemed to be valid when the interpretative community agrees it is valid. Such agreement is vital, for there is no objective criteria by which to judge the validity of a given interpretation apart from the assent of the interpretative community from which it emerged. The motor that drives biblical scholarship is not verification (which is usually unattainable) but persuasion: scholarship advances when proponents of one theory manage to present their case in such a way that adherents of a different theory will find acceptable and compelling. Each party must try to convince the other, and when one party succeeds there is no higher court of appeal to which the outcome might be referred than the assent of the interpretative community. In this way, fanciful or idiosyncratic interpretations will be ruled out of court, for the interpretative community will generally have little difficulty in deciding where the area of legitimate interpretation ends and where fanciful speculation begins. It is therefore in the interest of all interpreters of the Bible to produce readings that are plausible, for if there is no group or community that is persuaded by a given interpretation, that interpretation will simply not survive. If the reader of the Bible is a biblical specialist, his or her interpretation will be analysed, discussed and adjudicated by the community of scholars of which he or she is a part (represented, perhaps, by such illustrious professional societies as the Society for Old Testament Study or the Society of Biblical Literature); if the readers are members of a church or synagogue, their interpretation will similarly find acceptance or rejection within the religious community of which they are part.

The notion of the 'interpretative community' thus places some common-sense restrictions on the activity of readers of the Bible and allows them to tread the delicate path between subjectivity and objectivity. On the one hand, it rejects the notion that interpretation is a completely mechanical activity and that 'meaning' is just a property of the text, merely waiting to be discovered; on the other hand, it is not entirely discretionary, allowing readers to discern whatever meaning they please in a text, according to the whim of the moment. Interpretation is not completely mechanical, but nor is it completely arbitrary, for the interpretative community is always there to ensure that the Bible is read in agreed, controlled, non-arbitrary ways. There is thus a relocation of interpretative authority from the author/text to the community of readers who will exercise a kind of censoring activity, accepting certain readings as normative and rejecting others as untenable.

Thus the fears raised by some biblical scholars that the application of reader-response criticism to the discipline will only result in an unbridled subjectivity or in an infinite variety of unstable readings, although understandable, are unfounded, for the interpretative community will always serve as a safeguard against the dangers of excessive interpretative freedom. Readers of the Bible will have their reading experience shaped by the community of which they are members and – aware of their responsibility to the corporate enterprise – they will be constrained in their reading by their tacit awareness of what is and what is not a reasonable thing to say. There is thus no reason to suppose that the application of reader-response criticism to biblical studies will result in an irresponsible eclecticism, for the interpretative community will provide a restraint upon interpretations that are whimsical and irresponsible and will ensure that individual fancy will eventually give way to general acceptance.

At this point, it may be useful to illustrate how reader-response criticism functions in practice in relation to the Bible, and in what follows we focus on the way reader-response critics might approach the gospel of Mark.

Reader-response criticism and the gospel of Mark

Traditionally, studies of Mark's gospel have focussed on the intention of the author, or the historicity of the events he records, or the particular theological or Christological emphasis of the work. Reader-response critics, on the other hand, are more inclined to focus on the temporal experience of reading rather than on the static structure of the text. How does the author of the gospel manage to manipulate the reader to share his point of view? How does he lead the reader to fill in the gaps in the text and resolve the questions that remain unanswered in the course of the narrative? How does he use irony to drive his point home?

It will be convenient to begin by considering the familiar story of the feeding of the multitude in Mark's gospel.[15] Mark, in fact, contains two accounts of miraculous feeding: in the first narrative, contained in 6.30–44, Jesus feeds 5,000 people in a 'deserted place' with five loaves and two fish, while in the second account, in 8.1–10, Jesus feeds 4,000 people with seven loaves and a few fish. In the first account, the disciples are represented as having no idea how such a vast throng could be fed with such meagre provisions and, as readers, we find ourselves sympathizing with them in their predicament and fully understand why they ask Jesus, in all innocence, 'Are we to go to spend two hundred denarii to provide them with food?' (6.37). However, when we read a couple of chapters later that the disciples are faced with a virtually identical situation and still cannot fathom how Jesus could feed such a multitude, we cannot but be surprised by their lack of insight, and our sympathy begins to give way to annoyance. After all, if we, as readers, can remember the first feeding episode why, we wonder, could they not? What has happened here is that the narrator has manipulated us into a position of knowing more than the disciples, and he has manoeuvred us into passing an unfavourable judgement on them. The inclusion of two similar feeding stories is no longer viewed as a botched job by an incompetent author or editor who failed to realize that virtually the same story had been included twice in the same gospel; rather, the repetition is regarded as a rhetorical strategy deliberately deployed by the narrator to emphasize the stubbornness and lack of understanding of the disciples who seemingly have learnt nothing from past experience.[16]

Our view of the disciples' stubbornness and obtuseness is confirmed as the gospel story progresses. Mk 8.22–6 and 10.46–52 contain two stories about the healing of a blind man, and in between these narratives Jesus repeatedly teaches his disciples about the path of service and suffering that he is following, but they fail to understand the significance of his words. Indeed, while Jesus was predicting his impending suffering and death, his disciples, with crass insensitivity of his fate, are found debating among themselves who would be the greatest (9.34). We now begin to sense an ironic tension between the sight achieved by the blind men and the stubborn, persistent blindness of the disciples. Even having witnessed two miracles of feeding and been privy to Jesus' teaching the disciples still do not 'see' Jesus for who he really is! The narrator is manipulating us to distance ourselves from the disciples and align ourselves with Jesus. We are actually closer to Jesus than his own disciples were! As the gospel proceeds, the disciples gradually regress further in insight and understanding and become increasingly removed from Jesus until, at the end, the distance between them has become total and they betray, deny and abandon him in his hour of need. Now, if we were to ask (with Stanley Fish) 'What does this text *do*?' the answer is plain: the gospel invites us, as readers, to assume the mantle of discipleship and challenges us to remain faithful even as the original disciples of Jesus had failed to live up to their calling.

As readers of Mark's gospel, we are drawn into the narrative not only by what the text spells out but also by what it withholds. We are invited to fill in the 'gaps' in the text and to infer what is not explicitly stated. As we have seen, by 'gaps' or 'indeterminacies' Wolfgang Iser meant a lack of continuity between different parts of a text; in the linear process of reading there is a movement from one literary unit to another and it is up to the reader to bridge the 'gap' between the units. Mark's gospel provides a paradigm example of a text which is replete with 'gaps' that we, as readers, are expected to fill in. The most obvious 'gaps' are those between different episodes which are frequently juxtaposed to one another without any clear linkage between them. For example, in Mk 3.19–35, Jesus is teaching in a house but is then abruptly encountered teaching by the sea (4.1). In this case, the reader must fill in the gap and subconsciously visualize the physical movement of Jesus from one location to another. Matthew (one of the earliest readers of Mark's gospel) helpfully fills in the gap for us by informing us that Jesus, the same day, 'went out of the house' and sat beside the sea (Mt. 13.1). Another example may be found in Mk 3.1–6 where Jesus heals a man in the synagogue on the Sabbath, an action that induces the Pharisees and Herodians to plot against him; then, suddenly, in 3.7 we find Jesus by the Sea of Galilee healing many people (3.7–12). Again, the reader is expected to fill in the gap in the text: was there a connection, we wonder, between the plot against Jesus and his withdrawal to the sea? Here, too, Matthew fills in the gap by removing any doubt: 'When Jesus became aware of this, he departed' (Mt. 12.15). A third example may be found in Mark's account of the resurrection of Jesus. Unlike the other three gospels, Mark's account ends with the empty tomb and nothing is said about the subsequent appearances of Jesus to his disciples. As Fowler has remarked, this is 'a narrative gap par excellence' (1996: 154). While biblical scholars have long debated the abrupt ending of Mark's gospel and regarded it as probably due to an accidental scribal omission, reader-response critics argue that the inconclusive ending is there for a purpose: the empty tomb awaits the fulfilment that only the reader can supply.[17] Similarly, when the women at the tomb are told to inform the disciples that Jesus is 'going ahead of you to Galilee' (Mk 16.7), readers of the gospel cannot be sure whether the women or the disciples will follow Jesus; they can only answer for themselves. Indeed, we are told that the women, having fled from the tomb, were so frightened that 'they said nothing to anyone' (Mk 16.8). The implication of Mark's gospel is that the story of the tomb was never told, but, as Fowler notes, this poses the reader with a challenge: 'The women may never tell the story of which they are a part, but the reader has read their story and can respond to it in a multitude of ways, among them the option of telling the story of the story that was never told.'[18]

As readers of the gospel we are also expected to hold seemingly disparate pieces of narrative together through prospection and retrospection; we are continually invited to look forward and back, constantly re-visioning what has already transpired and envisioning what lies ahead. Of course, as readers, we know what will happen in the story before it transpires, partly because it is already well known to us and partly because of the clear predictions within the gospel itself. Thus, when we are told in Mk 14.10 that Judas went to the chief priests in order to betray Jesus, we realize that we had already been forewarned that this is what Judas would do in 3.19; when Peter denies Jesus three times in Mk 14.66–72, we immediately recall Jesus' prediction to this effect in 14.30; the use of the word 'again' at the beginning of the second story of the feeding the multitude in 8.1 is a clear signal to the reader to recall the earlier feeding miracle in 6.30–44.

We have already observed an example of irony in Mark's gospel in his juxtaposition of the miracles of giving sight to the blind in 8.22–6 and 10.46–52 with the dismal failure of the disciples to 'see' Jesus for who he really was. Another example may be found in the portrayal of the character of Peter in Mark's gospel. We are informed at the beginning of the gospel that when Jesus appointed the 12 disciples, he gave Simon the name Peter, and the reader will no doubt recall the play on the name Peter ('rock') in Matthew's gospel ('And I tell you, you are Peter and on this rock I will build my church'; Mt. 16.18). No doubt the name suggests in the mind of the reader a character that is solid, sound and dependable; however, the reader is soon disabused of such an assumption as he or she reads Mark's gospel, for Peter turns out to be anything but a 'rock': in Gethsemane he falls asleep and fails to keep vigil with Jesus although he had been told to 'remain here and keep awake' (14.32–42), and in the trial scene he denies any knowledge of Jesus three times (14.53–72). It is as though the narrator is giving the reader a wink and saying: 'Look how unsteady and unreliable the so-called "rock" has proved to be!'

Another example of irony in the gospel occurs in the crucifixion scene. Here, the bystanders at the cross mock Jesus saying, 'Let the Messiah, the King of Israel, come down from the cross' (15.32). Of course there is here, in a sense, a double irony, for the mocking taunt of the chief priests and scribes is intended ironically; but for readers of the gospel there is another irony here, for what is clear to them, but hidden from the characters in the story, is that their mocking words are true! They utter a title for Jesus that they believe to be false but, ironically, from the perspective of the narrator and his readers the title describes precisely who Jesus is!

Examples of how reader-response criticism enriches our experience of reading the gospel of Mark could easily be multiplied, but the above examples are sufficient to bring about a heightened awareness of the narrator's skill and dexterity in constructing his narrative. It also highlights our own role as readers and suggests an element of collusion between the author and ourselves of which we may previously not have been entirely aware. Reading the gospel thus becomes an eminently satisfying experience, for the author has not only provided us with questions to be answered and challenges to be overcome but also has magnanimously assumed our capacity for dealing with the intricacies of the text which he has placed before us.

Conclusion

Biblical scholarship has always been enriched by a close engagement with other disciplines, and the present chapter has outlined how the phenomenon known as reader-response criticism has been appropriated by biblical critics who are anxious to move away from the predominantly 'historical' approach to the biblical text. Of course, in many ways, the application of reader-response criticism to the study of the Bible undermines some of the most cherished principles of established biblical scholarship. In the first place, it casts doubt on the possibility – and desirability – of an objective, dispassionate exegesis of the biblical text and recognizes that all interpretation is filtered through the reader's own subjective categories. Moreover, it questions the wisdom of seeking the 'original', 'true' or 'definitive' meaning of the text, preferring instead to contemplate the existence of a wide spectrum of possible alternative readings. Further, by placing such emphasis on the role of the reader, the biblical interpreter is encouraged to engage in a personal encounter with the text and to consider how it might be made meaningful and relevant to contemporary concerns. Biblical scholars in the more traditional mould are bound to harbour certain misgivings concerning the application of such an approach to their discipline, but there can be no doubt that reader-response criticism can prove instructive and illuminating for those engaged in the study of the Bible.

To some extent, reader-response criticism is about bringing a heightened awareness of what we have been doing all along as we were reading the Bible, but in doing so it has enabled us to appreciate the text in new ways and to achieve new insights. Our reading of the gospel of Mark has demonstrated how reader-response criticism can serve to enrich our understanding of a familiar story. As readers, we are privy from the outset as to the true nature of Jesus, for the very first verse proclaims him to be the Son of God. To the characters in the subsequent narrative, however, his identity remains largely a mystery, and as readers we can only wonder at the confusion and misunderstanding exhibited by those who came into contact with him. The gospel is designed to guide, direct and illuminate its readers, but at the same time it challenges them to resolve puzzles, to smooth out incongruities, and to respond to unanswered questions. Of course, the ultimate question raised in the gospel is the one posed by the disciples during the stilling of the storm: 'Who then *is* this?' and on the basis of the clues and signposts provided in the course of the narrative, each reader is invited to answer the question in his or her own way.

CHAPTER TWO

Feminist biblical criticism

Feminism is not just a theoretical world view or perspective but a women's liberation movement for social and ecclesiastical change.

Elisabeth Schüssler Fiorenza

The need for a feminist Judaism begins with hearing silence.

Judith Plaskow

Patriarchy is a many-headed monster, and it must therefore be attacked with all the strategies at our command.

Carol P. Christ and Judith Plaskow

Both the Bible and the history of biblical scholarship stand in need of feminist critique.

J. Cheryl Exum

It might be interesting to speculate upon the probable length of a 'depatriarchalized Bible'. Perhaps there would be enough salvageable material to comprise an interesting pamphlet.

Mary Daly

'Feminist biblical criticism' is a broad term encompassing a wide variety of methods and approaches, and feminist scholars range from those who reject the Bible altogether as an irredeemably patriarchal book to those who argue that the central message of Scripture is one of human liberation from all forms of oppressive structures. The aim of the present chapter is to outline some of the principal approaches adopted by contemporary feminist biblical scholars, and to consider the extent to which they have succeeded in bringing fresh insights into the interpretation of Scripture by challenging past assumptions and questioning past judgements. First, however, we briefly outline the beginnings of the feminist approach to the Bible and trace its development from the middle of the nineteenth century to the present day.

Feminist biblical scholarship: An overview

Modern feminist interpretation of the Bible can be traced back to the nineteenth century and to the work of such ardent feminists as Sarah Moore Grimké, Frances Willard and, perhaps most notably, Elizabeth Cady Stanton. In 1837, Sarah Moore Grimké, an active and dedicated advocate for the abolition of slavery, argued that legal discrimination against slaves was on a par with discrimination against women, and she laid the blame for both injustices squarely on the Bible. The subordinate position of women in society was, in her view, largely due to the 'false translation' of certain biblical passages and the 'perverted interpretation' of Scripture by predominantly male commentators. Grimké ventured to suggest, with characteristic understatement, that 'when we are admitted to the honor of studying Greek and Hebrew, we shall produce some various readings of the Bible a little different from those we have now'.[1]

Grimké and the early feminists were acutely aware that one of the reasons for the predominantly male bent of biblical scholarship was that universities and theological faculties were the preserve of male students; women were denied educational opportunities and consequently found it all but impossible to influence the shaping of religious academic discourse. Not only was the biblical literature itself male-dominated but so were the academic institutions in which it was studied. As a result, women found themselves in the unenviable position of being excluded not only from the biblical text but also from the process of its interpretation. There was a sense, therefore, in which they were caught in a vicious circle: the subservient role accorded to women in the Bible had resulted (among other things) in their exclusion from theological training, and the effect of that exclusion was that biblical interpretation had remained resolutely in the grasp of male commentators and male theologians.

The inequity of such a system was heavily criticized by feminists in the nineteenth century. For example, in 1878 Mathilda

Joslyn Gage, at the annual meeting of the National Woman's Suffrage Association, introduced a resolution that demanded the right of women to interpret Scripture, a right hitherto exercised only by men (Schüssler Fiorenza 1998: 60). A similar sentiment was echoed by Frances E. Willard, at one time president of the Women's Christian Temperance Union, who complained bitterly of the 'one-sided interpretation of the Bible by men' (1889: 37), and who urged young female scholars who possessed a modicum of linguistic competence to immerse themselves in biblical Hebrew and New Testament Greek, so that they might interpret the Bible 'in the interest of their sex' (31).

One of the first female scholars to call for a critical examination of the role that the Bible had played in the degradation of women in Western culture was the suffragist and women's rights advocate, Elizabeth Cady Stanton (1815–1902).[2] She claimed that the Bible, owing to its profound religious and cultural authority, had been instrumental over the centuries in establishing and consolidating the patriarchal exercise of power and in denying women some of their basic rights and freedom. Indeed, given that the Bible was primarily responsible for the denigration of half the human race, Cady Stanton could not understand why it was still held in such high esteem by women. Whenever they had complained about their lack of citizenship, or demanded equal access with men to theological training and to the ordained ministry, opponents of women's suffrage had used the Bible as ammunition against them: 'When in the early part of the nineteenth century, women began to protest against their civil and political degradation, they were referred to the Bible for an answer. When they protested against their unequal position in the church, they were referred to the Bible for an answer' (1895: 8). So deeply ingrained in the Western psyche was its teaching that it was proving to be a formidable barrier to the development of female liberation, for it was regularly cited as divine authority for discriminating against women and for justifying their subordination to men.

It was this realization that prompted Cady Stanton, towards the end of the nineteenth century, to initiate her ambitious project, entitled *The Woman's Bible*, much to the indignation of the church and, indeed, the community at large. The aim of this ambitious project was to highlight the male bias of Scripture and to excise from the Bible those passages that were blatantly misogynistic. Stanton defended her strategy of eliminating from the Bible texts that might offend female sensibilities in the following terms: 'We need an expurgated edition of the Old and the New Testaments before they are fit to be placed in the hands of our youth to be read in the public schools and in theological seminaries, especially if we wish to inspire our children with proper love and respect for the Mothers of the Race' (1898: 184). Stanton invited distinguished female biblical scholars versed in biblical criticism to contribute to the volume, reminding them that 'your political and social degradation are but an outgrowth of your status in the Bible' (1895: 10). However, much to her disappointment, most declined the invitation, 'afraid that their high reputation and scholarly achievements might be compromised by taking part in an enterprise that for a time may prove very unpopular' (1895: 9). Some of those invited objected to the project on the ground that biblical interpretation was irrelevant and they felt that their efforts would only prove to be a useless expenditure of energy, since the Bible had patently 'lost its hold on the human mind' and was little more than an account of 'the history of a rude people in a barbaric age' (1895: 13). Others refused the invitation on the ground that the project undermined their deeply-held belief in the inerrancy of Scripture, for they regarded it as a specially privileged source that was not readily amenable to the rationalistic methods of interpretation advocated by Cady Stanton.

Despite these setbacks, however, *The Woman's Bible* eventually appeared, in two volumes, in 1895 and 1898, and it contained a compilation of all the sections in the Bible which were of particular relevance to women, accompanied by an appropriate, often acerbic, commentary, usually written by Cady Stanton herself. Although the volume, once it appeared, was severely criticized by some – not least because of its perceived racist overtones[3] – one can only admire the sheer undaunted ambitiousness of the project which was the product of unflagging and unswerving labour by a scholar, already in her 80s, working without significant collaboration or institutional support.

The pioneering work of female biblical scholars such as Elizabeth Cady Stanton was greeted with considerable reserve by the male scholarly establishment, and consequently progress in feminist criticism of the Bible was painfully slow. When the American Society of Biblical Literature was founded in 1882 no women were among its members, and by the turn of the century there were only five female biblical scholars out of a total membership of 200.[4] The earliest female members did not deliver papers to the Society, nor did they publish articles in the Society's prestigious journal. Only in the second decade of the twentieth century did women begin to make serious contributions to the academic study of the Bible, and even then their contributions were never self-consciously 'feminist'. During the first half of the twentieth century, gender issues were evidently not regarded as acceptable topics for scholarly delibera- tions, and consequently feminist biblical studies remained at the periphery of academic discourse (Bellis 2000: 24–5). They were generally regarded with an element of disdain, and viewed as lit- tle more than a quixotic indulgence in a harmless, but ultimately irrelevant, hobby-horse.

Such a view, however, changed dramatically during the latter half of the twentieth century. The resurgence of the women's move- ment in the 1960s not only revived women's struggle for political and civil rights but also gave rise to feminist biblical studies as a new and exciting intellectual discipline. Volumes such as Phyllis Trible's *God and the Rhetoric of Sexuality* (1978) and the anthol- ogy *Religion and Sexism* (1974) edited by the Roman Catholic theologian Rosemary Radford Ruether, introduced many women to the new possibilities opened up by feminists for reading and understanding the Bible. These works may be regarded as marking the beginning of the 'second phase' of feminist biblical scholar- ship, the first phase having culminated, to all intents and purposes, in 1898, with the publication of Cady Stanton's work (Milne 1997: 40–1). During this 'second phase', interest developed in what it might mean to read the Bible self-consciously as a woman, and how women in communities of faith should respond to the patriar- chal emphasis of Scripture. While it was true that feminist biblical scholars still struggled to have their work published in the tradi- tional scholarly journals, it was becoming increasingly clear that feminist biblical interpretation could no longer be shunted to the edges of academia and be regarded simply as a passing fad. Indeed, by the late 1970s, feminist studies had become a recognized area of biblical inquiry and were included in the curricula of many univer- sities and theological seminaries. Since then the output of feminist biblical scholars has been nothing short of prolific, and sympathy for the type of approach that they advocated has steadily grown within the scholarly guild.[5]

Although some feminist biblical scholars such as Elisabeth Schüssler Fiorenza have complained that the 'woman question' continues to be neglected in what she calls 'malestream' biblical scholarship, and that anyone identified with the feminist cause continues to be professionally discredited,[6] the fact is that feminist study of the Bible has by now become a significant area of modern research. One indication of the popularity of the discipline is the wealth of 'feminist companions' to the Bible which have appeared from the press, and the influence of feminist biblical criticism is clear from the fact that standard works of reference on the Bible and biblical interpretation now include articles on 'feminist theology' as a matter of course. Significantly, when Carol Newsom and Sharon Ringe published in 1992 *The Women's Bible Commentary* (the title of which was a tribute to Cady Stanton's work a century earlier), there were enough female scholars to provide analysis of the relevant passages of every book in the Bible.

Feminist scholars recognize that there are serious issues in the Bible which must be addressed and profound questions that must be answered. How should women in the twenty-first century react to the repressive aspects of the biblical text? How should they broach a document that appears to legitimate patriarchal structures of domination and reinforce cultural stereotypes? How should they respond to texts that are regularly cited to emphasize the female 'virtues' of silence and submissiveness? We shall now turn to consider three different approaches advocated by contemporary feminist scholars who have attempted to address these issues.

The rejectionist approach

The main proponent of this approach is Mary Daly, whose controversial volume, *Beyond God the Father: Toward a Philosophy of Women's Liberation,* appeared in 1973.[7] Daly encouraged feminists to abandon the Judaeo-Christian legacy perpetuated by men and to form, instead, a new post-Christian faith capable of overcoming the evil of patriarchy and its predominantly negative power and influence. Daly argued that patriarchy was not some separate attribute of Judaism that could be purged from the Bible; rather, it was an intrinsic characteristic of biblical faith and was something that was woven into the very fabric of ancient Israelite society. Thus, as far as Daly was concerned, it was not a question of rejecting some aspects of the biblical text (such as its androcentric language) or eliminating particular passages that women might find offensive (such as the command for them to be subservient to their husbands; see Ephes. 5.22–4); it was, rather, a rejection of the Judaeo-Christian tradition in its entirety, since the Bible as a whole represented 'a universe of sexist suppositions' (1973: 5). For this reason, Daly believed that no one who was truly a feminist could find any authentic meaning for herself within the context of Judaism or Christianity, since the Bible, over the centuries, had proved to be damaging to women's interests and had been instrumental in keeping women within their allotted place in society. The biblical image of God the 'father' in 'his' heaven ruling over 'his' people was the quintessential product of a patriarchal mentality, and the core symbols associated with God had clearly been moulded by a male perspective. The psychological ramifications of this symbolism were immense, for it conditioned people to believe that it was perfectly in accordance with the divine plan that society as a whole should be male-dominated, and this inevitably had the unfortunate effect of legitimizing women's social and religious subordination. The Bible had effectively programmed them to be subservient to male authority and had thwarted all desire on their part to improve their status. The solution to such programming, however, was not to attack or undermine the biblical concept of God, but to abandon it altogether and search for new forms of religious experience that might be more congenial to the feminist agenda. Attempts to study the Bible in order to exonerate it of some of its more oppressive statements were regarded as at best a waste of time and at worse a noxious collaboration with the enemy.

The search for a new form of religious experience, radical though it might appear, seemed to Daly a natural and logical way forward, for although many women had abandoned all institutional forms of religion (or been abandoned by them), Daly believed that women in general still retained a deep spiritual yearning. Such yearning, she believed, could only find fulfilment in an exclusively female articulation of religious experience represented by the 'cosmic covenant', which involved coming into living harmony with the self, the universe and God. This transcendent dimension of feminism opened up human consciousness to the desire for a non-hierarchical and non-oppressive society and revealed sexism as the ultimate source of oppression. Without the inspiration of this vision there could be no social change, for it was this vision that enabled women to come of age and to rise above the false dualisms of this world.

Daly's radical proposal, however, has generally been regarded as too extreme, and few even among the most ardent feminists would want to reject the Bible in its entirety. Many feminists regard the biblical faith as an integral part of their identity and experience, and have no wish to relinquish their biblical roots or disown their religious heritage.[8] Far from rejecting the Bible, they want to preserve its legacy, even if that means reinterpreting and transforming the tradition from within. To disown the Bible completely was regarded as irresponsible, for – whether one was prepared to acknowledge it or not – the Bible continued to exercise considerable influence on society, and was still read and preached as an authoritative text in countless communities of faith. To repudiate the biblical tradition was effectively to disenfranchise oneself from the debate regarding the relevance and authority of Scripture. Besides, most feminist biblical scholars believed that they would win more converts by remaining in the struggle rather than jumping ship and rejecting the religious tradition *en bloc*.[9] Despite its patriarchal ethos, the Bible contained much of lasting and universal value that was worth salvaging, and simply to reject it wholesale was a classic case of throwing the proverbial baby out with the bathwater. The Bible could be explored by women for its liberating insights and could prove to be a useful weapon in the perennial struggle against patriarchal oppression. As Schüssler Fiorenza observed, the rejectionist approach failed to recognize that Scripture had been used not only to serve the interests of women's oppression but also to authorize and energize women in their struggle for emancipation (1983: xviii–xx; 1998: 26–8). Just as liberation theologians discovered in the Bible texts that were helpful in their battle for political and economic freedom, so feminist biblical scholars might find in it passages that could provide a resource for hope and encouragement in their own struggle for liberation.

Moreover, many feminist biblical scholars felt that there was a rigid and unbending finality to Daly's approach (Osiek 1985: 98–9). It failed to recognize that both Judaism and Christianity were complex and pluralistic traditions that were continually changing and adapting to the needs of the present. To place feminism and Judaism, or feminism and Christianity, as phenomena in perpetual conflict with each other was misleading and simplistic, for these religious traditions were not 'givens' that Jewish and Christian feminists must either accommodate themselves into or completely reject outright. Being a feminist was by no means incompatible with being a Christian or a Jew, and it was simply misguided to believe that the biblical tradition must be either accepted or rejected as a whole. Feminist biblical scholars were not, as Daly seemed to imply, traitors to the cause who had unwittingly colluded with the enemy (men), nor were they wedded to a tradition that was intent on sustaining women's powerlessness and legitimizing their social and religious subordination. Rather, they were scholars who fervently believed that it was better to reform the past than to ignore it, and that it was possible to claim allegiance to the biblical faith without necessarily accepting the so-called sexist and patriarchal elements that it contained. Instead of seeking to jettison the tradition and relinquishing their faith, they preferred to reinterpret the Bible and re-appropriate its message in new and interesting ways.

The revisionist approach

A very different approach to that of Mary Daly was advocated by those who argued that the Bible should be taken seriously, and should not be dismissed out of hand as an irredeemably patriarchal book. Such scholars readily conceded that if the biblical text were taken simply at face value it may well be concluded that women did not play a particularly prominent part in history, and that they were generally regarded as subservient to their male counterparts; however, they argued that this was only because their role had been deliberately downplayed and marginalized by the biblical authors and by later redactors. The task of feminist biblical scholarship, as they saw it, was to embark on a systematic study of the neglected duties and functions of women in both ancient Israelite society and in the life of the Early Church, thus ensuring that their contribution was not completely obliterated from the biblical record. In order to achieve this aim, they tended to highlight the forgotten traditions of the Bible and to reinterpret texts that had been skewed or misunderstood by subsequent commentators down the centuries. By adopting this method, they claimed to find, within the admittedly patriarchal context of the Bible, strong counter-currents which affirmed women's strength and courage, and which testified to their inherent dignity and worth.

With regard to ancient Israel, Carol Meyers has been at the forefront of those who have questioned the claim that women played little or no significant role in the nation's history. She argued that the social reality of ancient Israelite society was far more complex than the written records suggest, and that women had their own sphere of power and influence which was not always made clear in the biblical text. Social and anthropological studies of peasant societies comparable to that of ancient Israel suggested that women in Old Testament times enjoyed a relatively high social status and that they were integrally involved in the economic, political, social and cultural affairs of the community. Within the household, also, the woman played a pivotal role, and Meyers concluded, controversially, that in such a society female power was every bit 'as significant as male power, and perhaps even greater' (1988: 176).

While Meyers adopted a historical approach to the Old Testament, other feminist biblical scholars favoured a more literary approach. Among modern feminist scholars, one of the leading advocates of such a strategy was Phyllis Trible, who likened her own approach to Scripture to the woman in Jesus' parable who persistently searched for a coin that she had lost (Lk. 15.8–10): 'Much as the ancient housekeeper of the New Testament, while possessing nine coins, searched for the tenth which she had lost, so we too, while acknowledging the dominance of male language in scripture, have lit a lamp, swept the house, and sought diligently for that which was lost' (1978: 200). Unlike Mary Daly, Trible believed that the Old Testament contained material that *was* worth salvaging, and that it provided a message that was both liberating and relevant for women in their continual struggle for emancipation. Instead of being overwhelmed by the negative aspects of Scripture, feminist biblical scholars should highlight its positive aspects; instead of berating the Old Testament for its unrelenting patriarchal emphasis, they should celebrate the fact that a female viewpoint has survived in the tradition despite all attempts to suppress it. Such a viewpoint, according to Trible, may be found in the book of Ruth, which extols women's initiative and independence in a male-dominated world, and in the Song of Songs, where the voice of the female, in contrast to that of her male counterpart, is direct, articulate, steadfast and enterprising, and where there is no suggestion of male domination or female subordination (1978: 144–99).

Other feminist biblical scholars, pursuing a similar literary approach to the biblical text, have drawn attention to stories in which women were the major focus of attention (see Lacocque 1990). They highlight such formidable figures as Miriam, the prophet (Ex. 15.20), who had the sheer chutzpah to reproach Moses for his exclusive claim to divine revelation (Num. 12.1–2); or Deborah, the military strategist and heroic leader whose presence on the field of battle was regarded as a guarantee of success (Judg. 4.4–16; 5.1–22); or Huldah, the prophet who was consulted by the king's emissaries and whose crucial decision led to Josiah's religious reform (2 Kgs 22.14–20). By focussing on such positive images of women, adherents of this strategy argued that the Old Testament was not entirely devoid of a female perspective, and while they recognized the overwhelming patriarchal stamp of Scripture, they believed that there were fundamental impulses in the biblical tradition that were representative of more inclusive ways of thinking. Such traditions, it was argued, served to 'undermine patriarchal assumptions and temper patriarchal biases, often challenging the very patriarchal structures that dominate the narrative landscape' (Exum 1985: 74).

Turning to the New Testament, feminist biblical scholars tended to highlight the influence of women in the ministry of Jesus and in the life of the Early Church. It was pointed out that Jesus first proclaimed his Messianic status to a Samaritan woman at the well (John 4.25–6), and women (along with the poor and marginalized) were represented as hearing and responding to the good news when the religious authorities appeared to reject it. Women were ascribed a leading role in the stories of Jesus' suffering and death and, significantly, he appeared first to women after the resurrection and commissioned them to relay what they had seen to the disciples (Mt. 28.9–10; Lk. 24.8–10). The inclusive nature of the 'Jesus movement' opened up the way for women to assume prominent roles within the Early Church, and Paul's letters indicate that women such as Prisca were able to function as a missionary side by side with the apostle (Rom. 16.3), and that women such as Phoebe could assume the role of a minister in the church (Rom. 16.1).

Perhaps the most notable representative of the revisionist approach with regard to the New Testament is Elisabeth Schüssler Fiorenza, whose influential volume, *In Memory of Her: A Feminist*

Reconstruction of Christian Origins, is regarded by many as a landmark in feminist interpretation of the Bible. The title of the volume is derived from the story recounted in Mk 14.3–9 where, much to the consternation of the disciples, an anonymous woman anoints Jesus with precious ointment, and he responds by saying that wherever the gospel is proclaimed throughout the world what she had done would be told 'in memory of her' (v. 9). Significantly, however, neither her name nor any details of her life have survived in the biblical record, and Schüssler Fiorenza regards this as symptomatic of the way in which biblical authors generally have deliberately contrived to erase women from the public memory. Since such traces of women's contribution have been forgotten, or deliberately suppressed by the biblical authors and editors, Schüssler Fiorenza regards it as only right and proper that women should be 'written back' into the texts where they are now virtually invisible. She observes that scholars have usually assumed that the Early Church was a 'man's church', an exclusively male cult, and that women were, at best, marginal participants in its activities and assigned a peripheral and subordinate role in its constitution; hence, Schüssler Fiorenza insists on operating a kind of 'reverse discrimination' by placing women at the very centre of the early Christian movement. Armed with the tools of historical criticism, she engages in what she terms a 'hermeneutic of retrieval' and attempts to highlight the *real* contribution of women, which the male-dominated text tries to keep hidden. By reading 'between the lines' of the text, she believes that we can glimpse a more positive role for women in the ancient sources than has hitherto been recognized, and that such glimpses reveal a 'struggle for equality and against patriarchal domination' (1983: 92). Schüssler Fiorenza insists that what the text represses or misrepresents should be as much our concern as what the text highlights and advocates; hence her attempt to break the silence of the text and to include the excluded. She explains her methodology in the following way:

> Rather than understand the texts as an adequate reflection of the reality about which they speak, we have to search for rhetorical clues and allusions that indicate the reality about which the texts are silent. Rather than take androcentric biblical texts as informative 'data' and objective reports, we have to understand them as social constructions by men and for men and to read their 'silences' as indications of the historical reality of women

about which they do not speak directly. Rather than reject the 'argument from silence' as a valid historical argument, we have to read carefully the 'clues' of the text pointing to a different historical reality and to integrate them into a feminist model of historical reconstruction in such a way that we can 'fill' out the silences and understand them as part of the submerged traditions of the egalitarian early Christian movement. (1985a: 60)

According to Schüssler Fiorenza, female subordination was not a part of the original gospel tradition but the result of the Church's eventual compromise with the patriarchal society of which it was part. The equality of men and women in the circle of Jesus' followers and in the Early Church was only eclipsed when the church eventually accommodated itself to the customs of the male-dominated Roman world. Working within that ethos, the editors of the New Testament documents had little incentive to extol women's participation in the early Christian movement; indeed, they may have deliberately downplayed women's role for fear that it might prove a threat to their own power, influence and authority. It was precisely because such male bias exists in the biblical tradition that we are now left with only vague hints in the extant texts of the egalitarian-inclusive nature of the early Christian movement; such hints, however, are regarded by Schüssler Fiorenza as significant, since they represent 'the tip of an iceberg indicating a possibly rich heritage now lost to us' (1985a: 59). Schüssler Fiorenza's aim is thus to look beyond the restrictive practices of the Early Church as represented in the New Testament and, in doing so, to try to make the submerged iceberg visible.

The type of arguments deployed by adherents of the revisionist approach, however, has been subject to much criticism. In the first place, it is generally recognized that our information about ancient Israelite society and the community of the early Christian church is very limited, especially with regard to the role of women; consequently, hypothetical reconstructions such as those advocated by Schüssler Fiorenza are bound to be, at best, tentative. She readily concedes that she is engaged in an 'imaginative reconstruction of historical reality' (1985a: 61),[10] but it is a moot point whether her reconstruction is imaginative or *imaginary*. Her basic presupposition may appear reasonable enough: if you cannot prove that women were *not* members of the 'Jesus movement' and did *not* participate in the life of the Early Church, you should give the benefit of the doubt to traces in the biblical text that suggest that they *did*. But such an argument from silence will not cut muster with the majority of biblical scholars, and it is surely at least conceivable that the historical marginality of women reflected in the biblical text was due not to the conspiratorial silence of the biblical authors and editors but to the fact that women *were* marginal in both the history of Israel and in the community of the Early Church.[11]

The reader-response approach

Feminist biblical scholars have long emphasized the importance of adopting an inter-disciplinary approach to the Bible, and some of the most exciting and innovative contributions of recent feminist biblical criticism have come from those who have embraced a reader-response approach to the text. As was noted in the previous chapter, the term 'reader-response criticism' refers to a diverse assortment of methodological perspectives, but one that has proved particularly helpful for recent feminist biblical critics is the approach known as the 'resisting' or the 'dissenting' reader (see Davies 2003). This approach takes its cue from the study by the literary critic Judith Fetterley, whose study of the 'resisting reader' was published in 1978, and is now commonly regarded as a classic of feminist reader-response criticism. Fetterley's aim was to examine the problem encountered by female readers reading male-orientated works of American literary fiction. She argued that the canon of classical American literature was thoroughly androcentric; it was written from a male perspective, imbued with male presuppositions, and intended for a predominantly male audience. Women who read this literature were thus conditioned to think as men, to embrace a male point of view, and accept as normal and legitimate a male system of values. The text solicited their complicity with its patriarchal ideology and persuaded them to view the male perspective as universal and the male experience as the norm.

Fetterley's observations clearly have resonance for female readers of the Bible, for they, too, are faced with texts written by male authors, texts in which the female perspective is muted if not altogether excluded. Like female readers of classical American fiction, female readers of the Bible are faced with an androcentric canon, and are invited to participate in an experience from which they themselves are often excluded. The male-dominated language of the Bible has the effect of making them feel invisible by subsuming them under masculine linguistic terms. For example, the Decalogue (as regards both grammar and substance) addresses the community only as the male heads of households; it is the male 'you' that is addressed by its commands, and women are absent or, at best, 'sub-indexed as male' (Brenner 1994: 255). Further, the basic symbols of the biblical faith – king, lord, master, father and husband – occur with such frequency in the Bible that the female reader almost inevitably finds herself internalizing such images and identifying with the male perspective. Such symbols encourage women to suppress their own identity and to see the world 'with male chauvinist eyes' (Daly 1973: 49).

For many feminist biblical critics, the most effective way to counter such patriarchal indoctrination is by adopting the method advocated by Fetterley, namely, by assuming an adversarial attitude towards the biblical text. Such a method can bear many names – 'ideological critique', 'oppositional criticism', 'reading against the grain', 'a hermeneutic of suspicion' – but its underlying assumption is that the act of reading should involve resistance to the dominant structures of power inscribed in the biblical text.

One feminist critic who has deployed such a strategy of resistance very effectively is Mieke Bal, whose reading of the book of Judges deliberately focuses on the insignificant, the trivial, the different – the very elements that the traditional, dominant readings have tended to suppress or exclude.[12] She attempts to change the perspective of the text and reverse the established priorities in its interpretation so that 'what is seen to be central will be marginalized, and what has been treated as marginal will become central' (1988: 2). Bal adopts what she calls a strategy of 'counter-coherence': the more something is repressed in the text, the more it needs to be highlighted; the more it is hidden by the author, the more it needs to be brought to the surface. The text of the book of Judges, for example, gives the leading parts to men, so Bal begins by focusing on the women; the biblical authors concentrate upon the heroes, so Bal dwells upon the victims; the narratives preserve the anonymity of the female figures, so Bal proceeds to give them a name (1988: 17; 1990: 19).

Such resistance clearly involves a radical departure from the way in which the Bible is customarily read, for, traditionally, readers have been conditioned to remain slavishly respectful to the text's claims, and to respond to its demands with uncritical obeisance. They have regarded themselves as passive recipients of the text, and have felt obliged to submit to its authority and to acquiesce in its value judgements. They have read – and frequently studied – the Bible with an untroubled admiration instead of with a restless questioning. The type of approach advocated by reader-response criticism, however, serves to remind readers that they have a duty to interact with the Bible and to read it in an openly critical, rather than in a passively receptive, way. Of course, such an approach inevitably raises the question of the authority of the Bible, and it is to this that we must now turn.

The authority of the Bible

Christian and Jewish feminist scholars, working within the constraints of their own religious traditions, have inevitably been faced with the thorny issue of the authority of the Bible, for they find themselves in the frustrating position of having to accept as binding and authoritative texts that appear to be incompatible with some of their deep-seated beliefs and fundamental principles. The predicament that they face is well expressed by Letty Russell: 'Are they to be faithful to the teachings of the Hebrew scriptures and the Christian scriptures or are they to be faithful to their own integrity as whole human beings?' (1985a: 137). Of course, some feminist scholars, such as Mieke Bal, have little or no interest in the issue of the moral, religious or political authority of the Bible, and are content to approach it merely as one of the most influential literary documents of contemporary culture. Others, such as Mary Daly, have simply rejected the Bible and, disillusioned by its oppressively patriarchal stance, have dismissed its authority as a non-issue.

But many – perhaps most – feminist biblical scholars write from a position within the church or synagogue, and steadfastly refuse to abandon the Bible despite the fact that it has been used over the centuries to legitimate the subordination of women within Western society. Thus, instead of rejecting the Bible, they attempt to defend its authority by pointing to texts which celebrate God's liberating action in history and which affirm his solidarity with the marginalized and oppressed. Scholars such as Letty Russell, for example, concede that there are passages in Scripture that are highly problematic for women but argue that, ultimately, the Bible's authority resides not in its blatantly patriarchal and misogynistic passages but, rather, in those texts that speak of the possibility of a 'new creation' that would be radically different from the past and present, a new creation that would see the restoration of justice and equality in the world. On this basis, Russell can affirm that 'the biblical witness continues to evoke my consent, even as I reject many of its teachings as well as its patriarchal context' (1985a: 140).

Other feminist biblical scholars have adopted a much more radical and controversial solution to the problem of the authority of the Bible. Schüssler Fiorenza, for example, argues that whatever diminishes or denies the full humanity of women cannot, by its very nature, be regarded as authoritative divine revelation; only those biblical texts that transcend their patriarchal time and culture can be regarded as truly reflective of the divine will. '*The* litmus test for invoking Scripture as the Word of God', she argues, 'must be whether or not biblical texts and traditions seek to end relations of domination and exploitation' (1984: xiii). According to this criterion, then, only the non-sexist, non-patriarchal and non-oppressive texts of the Bible have the theological authority of revelation. The task of feminist biblical scholarship is to evaluate texts for their liberating or oppressive content, and only those that serve to empower women should be proclaimed as authoritative.

Such an approach to biblical authority, however, has met with little support among feminist biblical scholars generally. Many argue that to reject as non-revelatory passages which happen to contain pronouncements that are uncongenial or offensive to the individual is hardly satisfactory, for on that basis readers can simply reject everything that appears in the Bible with which they happen not to agree.

Perhaps the most satisfactory solution to the issue of the authority of the Bible is found – ironically enough – in the writings of feminist scholars who advocate a 'resisting reading' of the biblical text. Such scholars frequently observe that reading 'against the grain' of the biblical text is not to undermine the Bible's authority, for the Bible itself often probes and questions its own values, principles and assumptions and thus, in effect, invites readers to critique its patriarchal stance. Rosemary Radford Ruether, for example, readily concedes that many passages in the Bible appear to provide a seal of approval on the existing patriarchal social order; however, she insists that there are other passages that contain fruitful resources for the critique of patriarchy and that these resources should be appropriated by feminist biblical scholars to emphasize the liberating, egalitarian aspects of biblical faith. According to Ruether, it is primarily in the prophetic literature that God's judgement on the present social order is most clearly articulated, for in such passages as Is. 10.1–2; Amos 5.24; 8.4–6, he is represented as condemning the injustices of society and vindicating the cause of the poor and oppressed. The feminist agenda is viewed by Ruether as a natural progression from this prophetic critique of social justice; it is merely that the injustice against which feminists inveigh is that perpetrated against women (1982: 59–66). Paradoxically, therefore, while patriarchy is undoubtedly encountered in the biblical text, it can be denounced by the central tools of the biblical faith, and in applying to the text of the Bible a 'hermeneutic of suspicion', feminist criticism merely 'continues the process of scriptural hermeneutic itself' (Ruether 1985: 122).[13]

The advantage of Ruether's approach is that the interpretative key for feminist biblical scholars in found within the canonical tradition itself. The biblical texts themselves witness a world-view in need of change, and the prophetic tradition provides the modern reader with a warrant to dissent from the teaching of the Bible, to quarrel with its ethos and to question its more dubious pronouncements. Ruether's approach, however, has two major drawbacks. In the first place, it is arguable that there can be no warrant for extending the general critique of oppression in the prophets to a critique of sexism and patriarchy that is not in the biblical text. Secondly, given the decidedly negative view of female sexuality encountered in many prophetic texts,[14] it seems strange to argue that feminist biblical scholars should seek to resolve the issue of biblical authority by taking a leaf from the prophetic books.

A more fruitful approach is that of Ilana Pardes, who focuses on the tensions that exist in the biblical text between the dominant patriarchal ethos and the female counter-voices that lie buried beneath the surface. Miriam's protest against the privileged status accorded to Moses, for example, was a blatant attempt to defy the secondary, subservient role into which she had been cast (1992: 6–12). Similarly, Michal's criticism of David for his unseemly behaviour in publicly exposing himself was an attempt to assert her own role and authority as his wife (2 Sam. 6.12–23). Of course, both women were duly punished for having the temerity to challenge accepted roles and oppose established hierarchies, but the significant element is that the anti-patriarchal perspective has been preserved, against all the odds, in the biblical text. There is a tradition of resistance to patriarchal domination within the Bible itself, and there is a sense in which feminist biblical critics can thus claim the authority of biblical faith to denounce its patriarchal agenda.

'Objective' scholarship

Feminist biblical scholars frequently make their own religious, social, political and ecclesiastical interests clear and transparent at the outset, and they are highly suspicious of the idea that critical study of the Bible is a completely objective, disinterested and value-free enterprise. This is not to say that feminist biblical scholars have abandoned the historical-critical method, merely that they have begun to question some of its outmoded assumptions, and have challenged its practitioners to be open about their prejudices and presuppositions.

Of course, the idea that our presuppositions can influence our scholarly conclusions is by no means new; indeed, as far back as 1957 Rudolf Bultmann had raised the issue in an article entitled 'Is Presuppositionless Exegesis possible?'[15] Bultmann himself answered the question with a resounding 'No!' arguing that all readings of the Bible were 'interested readings'. In recent years, however, it is primarily feminist biblical scholars and liberation theologians who have been critical of the idea that scholarly study of the Bible is a completely neutral, value-free and objective scientific method, and as if to emphasize the subjectivity of their own approach they frequently preface their studies by declaring openly their personal background or ideological interests. Thus, for example, Carolyn Osiek notes that

I belong to a large institutional church with an amazing amount of diversity in its membership and a firmly entrenched patriarchal leadership. Although that should not determine the direction of my critical scholarship, it inevitably affects my experience; and the two cannot be totally separated. (1985: 93)

In view of their avowedly subjective approach, it will come as no surprise that much of feminist biblical scholarship is apologetic in tone; indeed, it is often characterized as 'advocacy scholarship' or 'engaged scholarship', and Schüssler Fiorenza has argued that it is incumbent upon such scholarship to expose the injustices of race, class and gender. To remain 'objective' and 'detached' in the face of such injustice is simply not an option, for 'intellectual neutrality is not possible in a historical world of oppression' (1982: 33). Schüssler Fiorenza thus makes no apology for attempting to reconstruct the early Christian movement in a way that supports her own feminist agenda, for she regards her interpretation as a weapon in a continuous struggle against patriarchal domination.

Feminist biblical scholars have sometimes challenged their male colleagues to reflect critically on their own unconscious assumptions and institutional interests, for they are acutely aware that the task of the feminist critic is to 'call the Bible and its interpreters to accountability' (Trible 1985: 147). Male interpreters are invited to explore the male bias of their exegesis and to consider how their interpretation might have served to reinforce and consolidate patriarchal values. Feminist critics argue that, for the most part, male biblical scholars have shown little awareness that such a bias even existed. They had written under the guise of a studied neutrality, whereas, in fact, they had (albeit perhaps unwittingly) imposed their own interpretative gloss upon the biblical text.

The way in which supposedly 'objective' male biblical scholars have interpreted the biblical text in such a way as to promote their own patriarchal interests is well illustrated in Phyllis Trible's discussion of the account of the creation and fall in Gen. 2–3 (1978: 72–143). These chapters have commonly been regarded over the centuries as one of the mainstays of the argument for female inferiority and male supremacy, and even today they are 'widely adduced as a justification for misogyny' (Bal 1987: 104). Yet, despite the ostensibly negative portrayal of woman in this text, Trible argues that a detailed examination of these chapters reveals that they are not as sexist as is commonly supposed, for it is not the narrative itself that promotes male domination and

female subordination, but centuries of male-dominated interpretations of the text, interpretations that have become so familiar
that they are deeply ingrained in the collective psyche of readers
in the Western world. The basic lines of this interpretation of the
narrative are familiar enough: God created man first (Gen. 2.7)
and woman last (Gen. 2.22), the clear implication being that she
must be inferior or subordinate to him; woman was created for
the sake of man as his 'helper', suggesting that she was merely
his assistant or attendant (Gen. 2.18); and woman was created
out of man's rib (Gen. 2.21–2), a further sign of her derivative,
inferior status. Such a reading of the story, informed by centuries
of interpretation, has, according to Trible, virtually acquired the
'status of canonicity' (1978: 73), and for this reason an attempt
must be made to read the story without the blinkers of male preconceptions. She thus proceeds to refute, one by one, each of the
statements above. In the first place, she argues that the story of
the Garden of Eden begins with the creation, not of 'man', but of
hā-'ādām, an 'earth creature', formed from the dust of the earth
(Gen. 2.7). The 'earth creature' was not as yet identified sexually;
sexual differentiation took place only when the earth creature
'through divine surgery' (1995: 12) was made into two separate
beings, one female (*'iššā*), the other male (*'iš*; Gen. 2.21–4). Man
and woman were thus given sexual identities at the same time and
not one as a consequence of the other's prior existence; thus their
creation was 'simultaneous, not sequential' (1978: 98). Further,
the fact that woman was created as a 'helper' (Gen. 2.18) was not
an indication of her inferior status, for the word 'helper' (*'ēzer*) is
often used in the Old Testament of God as the one who sustains
and delivers his people (see Ex. 18.4; Deut. 33.7). Thus, far from
implying inferiority, the word, if anything, connoted an element
of superiority, though Trible concedes that in the present context it probably indicates a relationship of mutuality and equality. Moreover, the woman was created not from the rib of man
but from the rib of the sexually undifferentiated 'earth creature';
hence woman is 'no opposite sex, no second sex, no derived sex –
in short, no "Adam's rib"' (1978: 102). Trible's point is that once
we go behind the traditional androcentric interpretation of Gen.
2–3, a story commonly regarded as imbued with chauvinistic ideas
is shown to betray a surprisingly egalitarian concept of the role of
the sexes.

Trible's interpretation of the Genesis narrative is not without exegetical difficulties, and it must be conceded that it sometimes smacks of special pleading. As Ilana Pardes has remarked, in Trible's hands 'the Bible almost turns into a feminist manifesto, where every detail suspiciously ends up supporting woman's liberation' (1992: 24). Nevertheless, the importance of her study is that it demonstrates how generations of male commentators have imposed their own interpretative gloss on the text, while ostensibly providing an objective, neutral, value-free exegesis.

Womanist criticism

Recent years have witnessed the emergence of 'womanist' criticism of the Bible, which is particularly associated with African-American scholars, and which represents a concerted movement away from the European and Euro-American perspective that has tended to dominate traditional feminist biblical criticism.[16] These scholars argue that the white, middle-class context of traditional feminist studies in the West has tended to make its proponents overly preoccupied with the issue of gender and oblivious to the equally important issues of class, race and ethnicity. White feminist biblical scholars had failed to see beyond their own narrow confines and had neglected the plight and interests of women who faced injustice and oppression not only on account of their gender but on account of the colour of their skin.[17] They had not taken sufficient account of the fact that individuals – irrespective of their gender – had been silenced, isolated and marginalized as a result of their ethnic identity. Womanist scholars pointed out that the Bible was not merely hostile to the dignity and welfare of women but that it had been used as an instrument of the dominant culture (of which white feminists were part) to subjugate African-American people and justify centuries of oppression. Thus the unremitting patriarchal emphasis of the Bible was merely part of a much larger problem which had not always been addressed by traditional 'white' feminist biblical critics. Hence, womanist criticism has frequently been very critical of the Eurocentrism of much traditional feminist biblical interpretation, and white feminists have been taken to task by their African-American counterparts for presuming to speak on their behalf. Renita J. Weems, for example, has been particularly scathing of the universalizing tendencies of North American and European feminist biblical scholars who 'homogenize women in general and women of color especially without regard to our differences of race, religion, nationalities, sexual orientation, and socio-economic backgrounds' (2006: 31). They had failed to realize that it was not simply the case that women read the Bible differently from men, but that women of colour read it differently from white women.

A good example of womanist criticism is found in Mukti Barton's interpretation of Numbers 12, a chapter that has been the focus of much attention by white feminist biblical critics (2006: 158–68). The chapter is regarded as significant for feminists because it describes how a woman, Miriam, along with her brother, Aaron, had the sheer effrontery to challenge Moses' claim to possess a special relation with God: 'Has the LORD spoken only through Moses? Has he not spoken through us also?' (Num. 12.2). In claiming to be Moses' equal in prophetic authority, Miriam acted with considerable courage, independence and initiative, and – not surprisingly – she is elevated by feminist critics as a glowing example of a woman who stood her ground and was implacably opposed to the hierarchical social structures of the time. On the other hand, the fact that Miriam, later in the chapter, is struck with leprosy and excluded from the camp for a period of seven days for showing such insubordination, indicates that the biblical narrator had little sympathy for female oppositional voices, and it is clear that in the power struggle between Moses and Miriam, the latter comes out as the loser. Barton, however, points to a feature of this story that is commonly neglected by white feminist biblical critics, namely, that Miriam also challenged Moses on account of his Cushite wife (Num. 12.1). Now the term 'Cush' can mean 'black' but in the biblical tradition it is commonly identified with Ethiopia (see 2 Kgs 19.9; Isa. 20.3, 5). Miriam could easily have pleaded for a role in the leadership of the people without playing the racist card, but the fact that she insisted on raising the issue of Moses' marriage to a foreign wife adds a significant dimension to the story. Traditional feminist scholars have, by and large, neglected the racist overtones of the chapter, and have focussed almost exclusively on the plight of Miriam and the issue of gender equality.[18] By overlooking the racial slur, Barton argues that they have demonstrated that their 'feminism is really White feminism' (166). While white feminists have drawn attention to the patriarchal bias of the text, Barton prefers to focus on the racial bias of the passage, and while white feminists have tended to identify with Miriam, applauding her sheer chutzpah in standing up to her brother, Barton, a woman of Asian origin, prefers to identify with the nameless Cushite wife.

Another biblical story, which has a particular resonance for womanist scholars, is the account in Gen. 16.1–16; 21.1–21 of the Egyptian woman Hagar and her Hebrew slave-owning mistress, Sarah. While traditional feminist scholars have tended to praise Sarah for acting decisively to protect Isaac's inheritance by having Hagar and Ishmael sent away (Gen. 21.10), womainst scholars would see the narrative in a very different light, for they are more likely to identify with Hagar, as regards her status, ethnicity and gender. As Renita J. Weems observes:

> It is a story of the social and economic disparity between women, a disparity that is exacerbated by ethnic backgrounds. It is the story of a slaveholding woman's complicity with her husband in the sexual molestation of a female slave woman. It is the story of the hostility and suspicion that erupt between women over the plight and status of their male sons. It is the story of an enslaved Egyptian single mother who is subjected to the rule of a vindictive and brutal mistress and an acquiescent master. It is a story familiar, even haunting, to African American female readers . . . [which] by way of a negative example, reminds such a reader what her history has repeatedly taught her: *That women, although they share in the experience of gender oppression, are not* natural *allies in the struggles against patriarchy and exploitation.* (1993: 44; her italics)

African-American female readers of the Genesis account are only too aware of the parallels between Hagar's plight and their own and, not surprisingly, they evince considerable sympathy with her predicament, regarding her as a sexually and economically exploited slave who is forced to run away and is eventually banished from the household.

Thus womanist scholars find themselves engaged in a battle on two fronts: not only do they have to oppose the male bias of traditional interpretation of the Bible (as white feminist biblical critics have done) but they have also had to contend with Eurocentric *feminist* readings that are often 'class-centered and ethnically chauvinistic'

(Weems 1993: 38). The cosy camaraderie of female scholars is undermined by the womanist approach, which insists that some *women*
have been responsible for the oppression of other women.

Conclusion

The last 40 years or so have witnessed a dynamic growth and development in feminist study of the Bible. The so-called woman issue,
often regarded in the past as a marginal topic unworthy of serious attention, is now a significant area of modern research. Owing
largely to the influence of feminist biblical scholars, inclusive language is now *de rigueur* in modern translations of the Bible and is
actively encouraged in scholarly publications generally.

As we have seen, feminist hermeneutics has embraced a wide
variety of methods and feminist biblical critics have opened up fresh
and stimulating ways of reading the biblical text that are not always
perhaps fully appreciated by mainstream biblical scholarship. They
have challenged the established intellectual framework of biblical
scholarship and encouraged scholars to declare openly their own
experiential presuppositions and institutional interests. In so doing
they have scuppered the myth of neutral, objective, value-free scholarship and have argued cogently that what makes scholarly analysis
of the Bible interesting are precisely the personal interests, perspectives and commitments that the individual brings to the biblical
text. Moreover, by insisting that the Bible cannot go unchallenged
if it is instrumental in legitimating the oppression of women, they
have raised profound questions concerning the nature and meaning
of biblical authority. Of course, feminist biblical criticism has not
been without its detractors, and womanist reflection on the Bible
has shown that the experience of white feminists by no means represents the universal experience of all marginalized persons. There
is clearly further room for dialogue between feminist and womanist
scholars, as indeed there is between Jewish and Christian feminist
scholars, between biblical and non-biblical feminist scholars, and
between all of these and mainstream biblical scholars, and the hope
must be that in future feminist/womanist criticism will become 'so
integral to strategies of interpretation that it is no longer distin-
guishable as a separate genre' (Loades 1998: 92).

CHAPTER THREE

Ideological criticism

Ideologues and fanatics have ideologies; our acquaintances have ideals; but you and I, friends, have reasoned convictions.

Wayne Booth

The study and writing of history, in short, is a form of ideology.

M. I. Finley

Only ideologists are always right; scholars know that everything they say is potentially wrong.

E. A. Knauf

Nobody would claim that their own thinking is ideological, just as nobody would habitually refer to themselves as Fatso. Ideology, like halitosis, is in this sense what the other person has.

Terry Eagleton

There is no innocent interpretation, no innocent interpreter, no innocent text.

David Tracy

Interpreting the Bible as an ideological document is a fairly recent development in biblical studies;[1] however, the last three decades or so have witnessed a veritable plethora of books and articles examining the ideological presuppositions of biblical texts.[2] Some scholars have focussed on the ideology of large tracts of biblical material (such as the Deuteronomistic History), while others have confined their attention to particular books or passages. The introduction of the term 'ideology' into biblical discourse, however, has not been universally welcomed. James Barr, for example, has argued that, with a few notable exceptions, 'the entry of the concept of ideology into biblical scholarship cannot be said to have been a happy event' (2000: 139). Barr does not, of course, deny that there is such a thing as ideology in the Bible and that the term may potentially be useful for biblical inquiry, but he argues that the way it has been used by scholars 'has been little short of chaotic' (139), for the concept has not always been 'properly analysed and clearly explained'.[3] Barr's criticism is not entirely unjustified, for the term 'ideology' has proved notoriously difficult to define, and explicating the nature and purpose of 'ideological criticism' in relation to the Bible has proved to be a difficult and complex task. Indeed, although 'ideology' has come to play a central role in biblical scholarship there is no uniform understanding of the term.[4] Some scholars have defined the term in a neutral way as referring merely to a set of ideas or a coherent system of beliefs (not necessarily true or false in themselves), which are characteristic of the values or world-view of a particular group, class or milieu. Others, drawing heavily on Marxist theorists such as Fredric Jameson (1981) and Terry Eagleton (1978), have tended to define 'ideology' in a negative, pejorative sense as referring to a set of false values (commonly designated 'false consciousness') or a system of illusory beliefs created by a social or economic system with the aim of presenting a distortive or deceptive view of reality.[5]

Ideology and power relations

According to some scholars, ideological criticism is an effective way of exposing power relations as they are expressed, albeit covertly, in the biblical text. David Clines, for example, argues that ideology arises from social conflict between various groups in ancient Israel, and since it is usually the victorious in any social conflict whose texts are preserved, the ideology encountered in the Old Testament is basically that of the élite and powerful in Israelite society (1995: 32–45). Clines supports his argument by referring to the laws of the Decalogue (Ex. 20.1–17), for he claims that, although these laws are commonly regarded as promoting the welfare of the community as a whole, they were actually promulgated to serve the sectional interest of particular groups in Israelite society. The laws themselves afford sufficient clues to enable us to discern who might belong to such a group, for it clearly consisted only of males (since the commandments are couched in the masculine singular form) and men who were wealthy (or at least wealthy enough to possess a house, slaves and livestock), middle-aged ('old enough to have working children but young enough to have living parents') and important enough to be called upon to give evidence in a lawsuit (Ex. 20.16). Equally significant are the groups *not* represented in the texts – women, children, slaves, the poor, the landless and the dispossessed. That these are sidelined, ignored or excluded from the Decalogue merely confirms that the Ten Commandments reflect the interests of the dominant group in society and that these laws were promulgated to defend the values of the ruling élite.

Clines' argument, however, has been criticized by James Barr, who contends that ideology arises not from social conflict but emerges naturally as a general consensus within the community. The view that the laws reflect the vested interests of a particular group in society is dismissed as lacking in evidence. Barr wonders, for example, in whose interests would the command in the Decalogue 'you shall not steal' (Ex. 20.15) have been promulgated? Are we to suppose that there was a 'pro-stealing party' whose interests were opposed by an 'anti-stealing party' and that the latter group emerged as victorious in this conflict? Such a view appears to Barr untenable, for it is by no means clear who the 'pro-stealing party' might be. It could hardly be thieves, since they would surely have been anti-theft, not wanting anyone to steal what they themselves had stolen! It seems far more probable in Barr's view that there emerged a general consensus in society that stealing was wrong and should therefore be prohibited (2000: 134–5).

But while an element of consensus would have been necessary for the laws to function effectively, such a consensus was probably achieved by means of ideological control. Laws favouring the rich and powerful were invested with a spurious air of naturalness and inevitability, which made them appear the very essence of common sense and normality. In this regard, the numerous slave laws contained in the Old Testament provide an interesting case in point, for such enactments were almost certainly imposed by the rich and powerful as a way of maintaining the status quo (see Ex. 21.2–11; Deut. 15.12–17). The concealed aim of these legal provisions was to defend the way in which people were socially constituted, and they were drafted in such a way as to persuade those in a state of dependence that they were extremely fortunate to be living under the protection of their wealthy masters. The slaves had, after all, been provided with meaningful employment and some measure of security, and although they had been deprived of their freedom their situation was surely infinitely preferable to that of the debt-ridden land-holders who were at the mercy of exploitative and unscrupulous money-lenders. The clear implication behind such legislation is that slaves should count their blessings and be grateful for being the recipients of such benevolence.

Naturally, the ideology present in such texts is all the more potent for being concealed. The need for such social stratification within society is presented almost as though it were a self-evident, universally accepted fact of life. The slave laws inculcated a belief that social injustices were inevitable or – preferably – that they were not *really* injustices at all. The text rationalizes the hierarchical system by providing a logical and credible explanation for its existence. It stood to reason that a society without masters and slaves would be intolerable – how could it possibly be otherwise? By means of such ideological conditioning, the oppressed became victims of a kind of myopic vision that prevented them from seeing the essential injustice of their situation. The ideology was presented in such a way that it had the effect of making the slave resigned, indifferent and unable to formulate criticisms or even to imagine an alternative system. The captives were thus reduced to a state of passivity, and became persuaded of the essential justice of the very social order that oppressed them. Moreover, as something of an added safeguard (lest anyone should have the temerity to question the fairness of such a system), the slave laws were presented as decrees issued by God himself, implying that such enactments must be regarded by all as timeless, absolute and authoritative. In this way, the legislation pertaining to slaves was made to appear immune to criticism or rational reflection, and the powerful were thus able to forestall any critical interrogation of the status quo.

Just as ideological criticism was an important tool to justify the hierarchical ordering of society with regard to the position of slaves, so it was also a valuable instrument to justify the position of the king. Royal ideology as reflected, for example, in the Enthronement Psalms (such as Pss. 96–9) and Royal Psalms (such as Pss. 2, 110) served to justify the role and status of the king, and to counter any threats from those who might want to usurp his position and claim the throne for themselves.[6] In order to quell any potential upheaval or factional dispute without having to resort to physical force or violence, such psalms emphasized the king's supreme authority and the inviolability of his position. He was, after all, the guarantor of

justice in his role as judge, and the guarantor of peace and security
in his role as warrior (Ps. 18.35–50).[7] Lest anyone be concerned
that such concentration of power in a single person might be misused in an exploitative or self-serving way, it was emphasized that
the king's authority would be exercised in favour of the weak and
oppressed, and that he had been commanded and empowered by
God himself to establish his justice and righteousness on earth
(Ps. 72.1–4, 12–4). Indeed, the king's functions in his earthly role
merely mirrored those of Yahweh in his heavenly role, and just as
any challenge to divine rule would shake the very foundations of
the earth, so any challenge to the king's position and authority
would bring about the gravest consequences for the entire people
of Israel. The sacrosanct and inviolable status of the king was further assured by his claim to be God's anointed who was privileged
to be seated at his right hand (Ps. 110.1) and who had been adopted
as his 'son' (Ps. 2.7). He thus possessed qualities and characteristics that set him apart from ordinary mortals, and this served as
a kind of divine legitimation of his position in the political and
social ordering of the state. Thus just as the laws governing slavery
gained an added authority because they emanated from God, so
divine approval was appealed to in order to safeguard the status
and role of the king.

Now it is not difficult to imagine which groups in society would
have been responsible for this ideology: it was, in all probability,
the rich and powerful who wanted a strong central government to
protect and legitimate their considerable economic and political
advantage.[8]

Ideology motivated by political interests

The narrative contained in 1 Sam. 14.52–2 Sam. 8.15 is frequently
regarded as a literary complex infused with political-ideological
interests, for the aim of these chapters appears to be to legitimize
David's acquisition of the throne once occupied by Saul.[9] That
the biblical author was concerned to glorify David's heroic status
is clear from the well-known account of the encounter between
him and Goliath, the champion of the Philistines (1 Sam. 17).
Doubts have long been expressed concerning the historicity of this
episode, partly because of the internal contradictions within the

Old Testament itself. While it is stated clearly in 1 Sam. 17 that it was David who killed Goliath, this appears to be contradicted by 2 Sam. 21.19, which claims that it was Elhanan, one of David's warriors, who killed the giant. This contradiction evidently presented the Chronicler with something of a conundrum, and a rather desperate attempt was made to harmonize the two conflicting accounts by claiming that Elhanan, in fact, killed Goliath's brother (1 Chron. 20.5)![10] Such relatively minor contradictions within the biblical narrative may seem trivial, but they are regarded by scholars as a significant indication of the *real* nature of the 'historical' sources of the Old Testament, for they suggest that the account of David's courageous act in 1 Sam. 17 was created for ideological purposes, namely, to elevate his heroic stature and to depict him as the chosen of God who was entirely worthy to occupy the throne (Garbini 1988: 22).

In the broader context of 1 Sam. 14–2 Sam. 8, the literary depiction of David's elevated status usually occurs at Saul's expense (see Brettler 1995: 101–9). Thus Saul's petrified reaction when faced with Goliath and the might of the Philistine army (1 Sam. 17.11; 28.5) contrasts sharply with David's bravery in fighting the giant single-handedly and even refusing to wear Saul's armour before engaging in the conflict (1 Sam. 17.38–9). Moreover, Saul's failure to defeat the Philistines in battle (1 Sam. 31.1ff.) contrasts with David's success in vanquishing Israel's arch-enemy (1 Sam. 18.5–7, 30; 19.8). Even when Saul does manage to gain some success when combating Israel's adversaries, the narrator is keen to emphasize the superiority of David's military prowess: 'Saul has killed his thousands, and David his ten thousands' (1 Sam. 18.7; 21.11; 29.5). Further, Saul is generally depicted in a way unbefitting a king: he orders his servant to kill the priests of Nob and proceeds to massacre the innocent victims of the city, including the men, women and children (1 Sam. 22.17–19); on the other hand, Saul spares the Amalekites, whom he should have killed in accordance with the terms of the 'ban' (1 Sam. 15; see Deut. 25.19). Indeed, Saul on more than one occasion, is depicted as attempting to kill David (1 Sam. 18.10–11; 19.1–2, 11–24) and even his own son, Jonathan (1 Sam. 20.33); by contrast, David, who had ample opportunities to kill Saul (1 Sam. 24.1ff.; 26.1ff.), steadfastly refused to harm 'the LORD's anointed' (1 Sam. 24.6; 26.11). Thus while Saul kills the innocent, David is depicted as sparing even the guilty. When

Saul eventually dies, the narrator appears to go out of his way to emphasize that David was in no way responsible for his death, nor was he complicit in the deaths of Abner, Saul's cousin, and Ishbosheth, Saul's son, as was abundantly evident from his reaction upon hearing of their demise (2 Sam. 1.11–16; 3.28–30, 33–7). Thus, far from attempting to usurp the reigning monarch, David is effectively exonerated of any guilt with regard to the downfall of the house of Saul.

The attempt to delegitimize Saul and assure the reader that the kingship was quite properly transferred to David is further highlighted by the narrator's insistence that the 'spirit of the LORD' was upon the latter (1 Sam. 16.13) and that God was unquestionably on David's side (1 Sam. 16.18; 18.12, 14). By contrast, it is clear that Yahweh had rejected Saul, for the divine spirit is depicted as having left him (1 Sam. 16.14) and, since he was no longer capable of receiving a divine oracle, Saul was pathetically forced to resort to necromancy, though he himself had earlier outlawed the practice (1 Sam. 28.3, 6–25). Of course, David's claim to kingship could not be legitimated genealogically, since David was not Saul's son, but the narrator manages to overcome this obstacle by subtly suggesting that a kind of pseudo-genealogical filial relationship *did* exist between them, and that David therefore had some kind of quasi-legal claim to the throne.[11] Thus Saul calls David 'my son' (1 Sam. 24.17; 26.17, 21, 25) and David calls Saul 'my father' (1 Sam. 24.11), and Jonathan, Saul's eldest son and rightful heir, is depicted as taking off his cloak and giving it to David (1 Sam. 18.4), a gesture which is usually taken to suggest that Jonathan was symbolically transferring his status to David, thereby making him a kind of surrogate son to Saul (Brettler 1995: 106–7). Indeed, Jonathan makes a pact with David and announces: 'You shall be king over Israel' (1 Sam. 23.17), thus effectively relinquishing his own right to the throne and acknowledging David as the legitimate heir. Indeed, even Saul is made to give voice to the idea that David had been designated to succeed him (1 Sam. 24.20). The climax of the pro-Davidic propaganda is found in 2 Sam. 7, where David is promised a perpetual dynasty and where his claim to the throne is regarded as having divine approval (vv. 13, 16).

The above discussion suggests that, far from attempting to provide a neutral or objective account of the past, the narrator has deliberately manipulated events to achieve a specific ideological goal, namely, to defend the assumption of power by the Davidic dynasty.[12] The positive portrayal of David in the literary complex 1 Sam. 14.52–2 Sam. 8.15 should not be taken to imply that the books of Samuel are devoid of an ideology favourable to Saul; on the contrary, 1 Sam. 1–14 portrays him in a predominantly positive light (Brettler 1995: 109). Thus, chapters 9–10 serve to confirm his divine legitimation, and chapter 11 praises his military prowess; by the same token, 2 Sam. 11–12 may be viewed as containing an anti-Davidic ideology, for he is here viewed as an adulterer and murderer who ignores his royal responsibilities by strolling on the palace roof looking at a beautiful woman while his army was fighting a battle against Ammon.[13] The conflict of ideologies within the text of 1–2 Samuel perhaps reflects the power-struggle between the Saulide and Davidic factions in ancient Israel, and it may be that the various events recorded in these books merely reflect the vested interests of particular movements within the community of ancient Israel. Be that as it may, the books of Samuel provide an excellent example of the way in which the biblical narrators could manipulate events in order to influence the attitudes and outlooks of their audience.[14] Inevitably, such a view raises questions as to whether 1 and 2 Samuel can be regarded as historiography in the proper sense of the term, or whether they should rather be viewed as literary compositions which, for ideological reasons, have been heavily edited for propagandistic purposes.[15]

Ideology motivated by religious interests

A classic example of this type of ideology may be found in the book of Judges, which is part of an extended work usually referred to as the Deuteronomistic History.[16] As many commentators have observed, a passage such as Judg. 2.11–23 is intended to function ideologically. A certain pattern emerges in this story which is repeated, with minor variations, in subsequent chapters: Israel commits 'adultery' by turning to worship other gods; as a punishment by God the people are oppressed by their enemies; in their misery they repent and cry out to Yahweh; he, in turn, is moved to pity, and raises a 'judge' to deliver them. With the death of each judge the same pattern begins anew. Clearly, the events recorded are ideologically contrived to teach the people about the dangers of apostasy and its dire consequences. While the tribes are faithful to Yahweh they enjoy peace and security in the land, but when they forsake him and turn to worship other gods they suffer defeat and are oppressed by the enemy. The message that the editors intended to convey could hardly be clearer: sin brings punishment, whereas repentance is rewarded with blessing. The reader is thus conditioned at the outset of the book (2.11–23) to understand the subsequent narratives in the context of the act-consequence nexus, though some of the stories themselves may suggest different readings. Of course, this is not to deny that the book of Judges may contain some accurate historical traditions, but the point is that these have been reworked and reorganized for a particular purpose, namely, to teach the readers a moral lesson.

Another example of ideology motivated by religious interests may be seen if we look again at the story of King David. As has been observed, the biblical account of his rise to power and subsequent reign is portrayed in 2 Samuel in a positive light – but only up to a point. After his adultery with Bathsheba and his unscrupulous behaviour towards her husband in 2 Sam. 11, nothing seems to go right for him or his family: the child born to Bathsheba dies (2 Sam. 12.15–19); his daughter, Tamar, is raped by her half-brother, Amnon (2 Sam. 13); and Amnon himself is murdered by his half-brother, Absalom (2 Sam. 13.23–33). This suggests a kind of measure-for-measure punishment of David and his family because he abused his royal power and status (Brettler 1995: 98–9). However, the story of David and Bathsheba is followed by an account of David's repentance (2 Sam. 12.13) and grief (2 Sam. 12. 15–23), and Yahweh's approval of the second child born of the union (2 Sam. 12.24–5). This fits in with the judgement/repentance theme which, as we have seen, is characteristic of the Deuteronomistic History.

But perhaps the ideological perspective of the Deuteronomistic editors is seen most clearly in their presentation of the fate which befell the kings of Israel and Judah. Little attempt was made to provide an objective account of their reign; on the contrary, the judgement passed on the various kings is based on whether they recognized the temple in Jerusalem as the only legitimate place of worship, or whether they permitted the people to sacrifice in the 'high places'. Hezekiah was one of the few kings who was regarded in a favourable light because he upheld the traditions of the Yahwistic faith: 'He removed the high places, broke down the pillars, and cut down the sacred pole' and 'broke in pieces the bronze serpent that Moses had made'; moreover, he trusted God and kept his commandments 'so that there was no one like him among all the kings of Judah after him, or among those who were before him' (1 Kgs 18.3–7). On the other hand, the kings of Israel are condemned out of hand, for they all did what was evil in the sight of Yahweh by 'walking in the way of Jeroboam and in the sin that he caused Israel to commit' (1 Kgs 15.34; 16.19).

Since the interest of the editors was expressly theological, they tended to overlook the political achievements of the monarch. A prime example of this may be seen in the attention (or, rather, the lack of attention) devoted to Omri in the book of Kings. From a strictly historical perspective, Omri was clearly a very important king, as is evident from the fact that the Assyrian annals referred to Israel for much of its subsequent history as the 'house of Omri'; yet, in 1 Kings, his reign is summarily dismissed in a mere six verses (16.23–8).[17] By contrast, over six chapters (1 Kgs 16.29–22.40) are devoted to Omri's son, Ahab, but this is not because he was more important politically or historically than his father, but simply because the editors were concerned with the religious repercussions of his marriage to Jezebel, which had the effect of introducing the worship of Baal into Israel. Thus there can be little doubt that the religious ideology of the editors had a major influence on their selection of material and on the way in which the various narratives were presented.

The Chronicler's account of history is similarly influenced by ideological considerations (Japhet 1989; Brettler 1995: 20–47). As in the Deuteronomistic History, the verdict passed on each king was based on the extent of his faithfulness to the Jerusalem cult. There is approval of those kings who 'did what was good and right in the sight of the LORD' (2 Chron. 14.2), and condemnation of those who 'did what was evil in the sight of the LORD' (2 Chron. 33.2). Kings who were commended were those who had been faithful to God, and who had striven to maintain temple worship and the purity of the Jerusalem cult; these kings were duly rewarded by being granted military success and material prosperity. That faithfulness to Yahweh brought in its wake divine blessing may be seen, for example, in the case of Abijah, who relied upon God and was consequently ensured success in defeating Jeroboam and the

Israelites (2 Chron. 13.19–20). On the other hand, kings who were proud, self-reliant and who had forsaken God were punished and inevitably suffered defeat in battle. Thus, for example, Jehoram, who had been unfaithful to Yahweh, saw his family and property being plundered by the Philistines and Arabs (2 Chron. 21.16–19), and he himself died as a result of an ignominious disease (2 Chron. 21.18–19). The religious ideology was clear for all to see: there was no disaster without guilt, no sin without punishment.

The above discussion suggests that the biblical authors and editors exercised considerable freedom in the way they selected from the sources at their disposal and in the way in which they rearranged and rewrote the material to serve their own purpose. They had their own agendas to promote, their own ideology to advance, and this inevitably shaped the way in which they presented the history of their people.

History or ideology?

The tendency to view the presentation of Israel's past as an ideological construction inevitably had considerable ramifications with regard to the historical value of the biblical narratives, for it was clear that the events recorded in the Old Testament had been modified, embellished and refashioned in order to accommodate the religious beliefs or political outlook of the various writers or editors. Such an emphasis on the ideological nature of the biblical material is a comparatively recent development in scholarly research, for until the early 1970s there was a general consensus that the texts encountered in the books of Samuel and Kings were, in essence, 'historical', at least in the sense of being a reasonably accurate depiction of ancient Israel's past. Ideological critics, however, argued that previous scholarly reconstructions of the history of Israel had amounted to little more than a bland acceptance of the biblical data, without subjecting the relevant texts to critical scrutiny. Little, if any, attention had been paid to the ideological character of Israel's understanding of its own past or, indeed, to the nature and purpose of the biblical writings in general. Once it was recognized that the biblical authors' account of the past was influenced by their religious and political ideology, the historical value of Old Testament narratives came to be viewed in a very different light, and much scepticism was expressed concerning the reliability of the events recorded. To complicate matters further, some of the biblical sources that had previously been dated in the ninth or eighth century BCE now came to be placed in the exilic or post-exilic age, and came to be regarded as the product of the ideology of these later times. Far from being an accurate record of the events they purported to describe, the biblical narratives merely reflected the ideology, outlook and aspirations of their authors. The matter was stated very succinctly by Giovanni Garbini, who argued that 'no historiography is ideologically neutral' and that 'every historical narrative reflects in a more or less veiled form a particular world-view' (1988: 14). Indeed, he even went so far as to claim that everything in the Old Testament was 'markedly ideologized and bent to the sole purpose of showing the truth of a particular religious vision' (1988: 61).

Such an argument inevitably meant that increasing emphasis came to be placed on the literary artistry of the biblical narrators and the creative ability of the biblical authors in shaping the material at their disposal, and consequently the narrative world of the Old Testament was regarded as a 'fictive' world which bore little relation to the 'real' world of Israel's past. That which had been regarded as 'history' by a previous generation of biblical scholars came to be viewed as an ideological construct created by the biblical authors to serve a particular purpose or to promote a particular agenda. Indeed, some revisionists, such as Philip Davies, went so far as to claim that the way in which 'historical' events were reported in the Old Testament had 'virtually everything to do with literary artistry and virtually nothing to do with anything that might have happened' (1992: 29). That being so, Davies refused to give biblical texts primacy of place in the reconstruction of the history of Israel; rather, the real 'history of Israel' was to be sought in the artefacts and inscriptions which the people left behind, for archaeological remains provided a more 'neutral' account than anything that might be gleaned from the textual material. Indeed, some even went so far as to claim that ideology was so pervasive in the biblical text that it was almost completely devoid of historical value, and that there never was a David or a Solomon, nor was there ever a united kingdom of Israel, or an exile or a return from Babylon. The entire Old Testament was nothing more than a religious ideology expressing itself in a form purporting to be historical narrative.

Such extreme views, however, merely show the slippery slope to which an excessive emphasis on ideology may eventually lead. While it may be readily admitted that no account of history is ever an entirely objective representation of reality, it is surely erroneous to assume that the presence of ideology in a work automatically disqualifies it from being considered historical. As James Barr has rightly observed, 'just as historical texts will commonly be ideologically slanted, ideological texts will commonly contain historical material' (2000: 82). The fact is we simply do not know to what extent the ideology of the biblical writers distorted their approach to social reality (thus producing a 'false consciousness') because we have no access to the social world of the Bible outside the biblical text (Carroll 1990: 309). Certainly, to dismiss the biblical texts completely on account of their ideological underpinnings and to rely instead on archaeological artefacts seems to be a very dubious methodological procedure, for the significance of such artefacts, of necessity, requires evaluation and thus cannot be regarded as providing a more 'neutral' account of the past than the biblical writings themselves.

Critique of ideology

The task of ideological criticism is not only to *unmask* the ideology of the text but to subject it to detailed critical analysis. This is by no means an easy undertaking, for the ideology is often presented in such a matter-of-fact way that it does not occur to readers to pause and question its underlying logic and assumptions. The ideology swathes them in the illusion that this is, indeed, the way things should be, and so convincing is its propaganda that they can hardly imagine how things could be any different. Readers thus find themselves taken in by the text's ideology, lulled into a state of passive acceptance, and seduced into accepting as valid and legitimate a set of values which, in their more guarded moments, they might reject, or at least question. Of course, it is a tribute to the success of the biblical authors that they have been able to manipulate their readers in such a way, for the job of purveyors of ideology has always been to persuade people to see the world as *they* see it and not as it is in itself.

Such is the power that the biblical text wields over the reader that even biblical scholars who pride themselves on being neutral and dispassionate observers often succumb (albeit perhaps subconsciously) to the text's blandishments and accept them as their own. David Clines has demonstrated how commentators on Amos generally take the prophet's point of view for granted and subscribe unthinkingly to his version of events (1995: 76–93). Amos' pronouncements are regarded as fair, just and inspired, and he is admired for his moral fortitude, whereas his opponents are assumed to be wrong, foolish and misguided, and are rightly condemned by the prophet for their corruption and depravity. Admittedly, Amos' words are powerful and persuasive, but how, as readers in the twenty-first century, should we respond to them? Are we going to 'abandon our moral repertory, with its sensitivities and uncertainties . . . and accede to the simple moral defeatism of an outraged prophet?' (Clines 1997: 27). This, in Clines' view, is precisely what most readers of Amos – and, indeed, most commentators on the prophet – have done. Instead of registering their disgust as they encounter ideologies which they deplore, they have been seduced into a readerly acceptance of the text. While we may conceivably agree with Amos that his contemporaries deserved capital punishment on account of their war crimes (Am. 1.3–2:3), they surely did not deserve to be shunted off to a foreign land simply because they had been lying on beds of ivory and eating the choicest foods (Am. 6.4–7). Instead of taking a step back from the text and critically questioning its assumptions, commentators have merged into empathetic harmony with the text's ideology and have all but accepted it as their own. Such is the complicity between the text and its readers that they have automatically conferred unquestioned moral authority upon the prophet and accepted without further thought his own version of the truth. But what if his opponents were right and he was wrong? What might the situation in Israel during the eighth century BCE have looked like if we had heard it from the lips of Amaziah, the high-priest, whom Amos condemns (Am. 7.10–17), rather than from the lips of the prophet himself? The fact is that everything is heavily stacked in Amos' favour; his account of events is seldom questioned, and his claims are rarely resisted. Seduced by generations of readerly co-operation with the text, commentators have generally been unable to free themselves from its clutches and have shown themselves incapable of rising above the miasma of its ideological smokescreen.

For this reason, ideological criticism serves as a salutary reminder that academic scholars must not only expound, explain and analyse the biblical text but also critique and evaluate it, and if they fail in this regard they have, in Clines' view, left 'half their proper task unattempted' (1995: 21).

Ideology and biblical interpretation

The study of ideology in relation to biblical studies has tended to focus on the ancient texts themselves with surprisingly little reflection on the ideology of those who have interpreted the biblical material.[18] Of course, scholars in the past have generally been loath to admit that their own readings are ideological, preferring to believe that they were writing under the guise of a studied neutrality. It is for this very reason that recent ideological criticism has been concerned to unmask not only the ideology of the authors of the Bible but also that of the interpreters of the Bible, and to challenge them to question the assumptions upon which their interpretation is based. At this point it may be helpful to note examples of how both New Testament and Old Testament scholars may have allowed their own ideological position to influence their interpretation of the biblical material.

With regard to the New Testament, we may briefly consider scholarly discussions of Jesus' teaching concerning wealth and poverty (see Míguez-Bonino 2006: 41–2). Even a cursory look at the biblical commentaries on the relevant verses in the gospels reveals an almost uniform interpretation of Jesus' teaching on this issue: riches in themselves are good, and far from condemning his followers for being greedy or rapacious in their accumulation of wealth, Jesus would have happily blessed their efforts at personal enrichment. Such is undoubtedly the message implied, for example, in the parable of the talents in Mt. 25.14–30 and in the corresponding parable of the pounds in Lk. 19.11–27, which imply that the person who has capital and uses it judiciously to make a profit will be rewarded with further commercial opportunities. But how can such teaching be reconciled with the beatitude in Luke's gospel where Jesus declares that it is the *poor* who are blessed (Lk. 6.20)? Commentators almost invariably conclude that Jesus could not in this instance have been referring to material poverty, and consequently the verse is interpreted in the light of the similar beatitude in Matthew's gospel (Mt. 5.3), where Jesus specifically refers to the poor 'in spirit'. I. Howard Marshall, in his monumental commentary on Luke, argues that it is the Matthean version of the beatitude that is probably original, for it 'brings out more forcefully the ethical and spiritual associations of poverty, and precludes the misunderstanding that might arise from the Lucan form' (1978: 250). The fact that the very next verse in Luke refers to the 'hungry' does little to undermine the view that Jesus was speaking in spiritual rather than economic terms, for the 'hunger' which he had in mind was conceivably a 'desire for spiritual satisfaction' (250). The 'woe' on the rich, which appears a few verses later in Luke, was uttered not because they had accumulated inordinate wealth but because they had been distracted by the spurious consolations of this world and 'saw no need to secure for themselves treasure in heaven by giving to the needy' (256). Of course, this is precisely the interpretation of Jesus' teaching which well-heeled readers in the West would welcome: Jesus would not have pronounced a blessing on those who lacked material possessions but may well have blessed those who felt themselves to be spiritually impoverished; similarly, Jesus would not have condemned those who accumulated material wealth, but may well have censured those who had become self-satisfied and indifferent to the needs of the poor.

Now it is reasonable to ask whether the socio-cultural and economic circumstances of those who have interpreted these passages have influenced the way they have understood the biblical text. Not surprisingly, interpreters from the Third World have a very different understanding of the Lucan passage. As Carlos Mesters has observed, those who are part of the basic ecclesial communities in Brazil, who find themselves impoverished by an oppressive capitalist system, interpret Jesus' words very differently. They believe that he was concerned with the *real* issues of poverty, hunger, misery and oppression, and the most obvious meaning of his words is that he was announcing a blessing on those who were materially deprived. Pious comments about having the 'right attitude' to riches and wealth cut little muster among those facing a life of poverty and injustice. As far as they are concerned, the rich are

condemned simply on account of their wealth, and no interpretative sleight-of-hand can make the text mean anything else. The
condemnation of the rich was uttered by Jesus precisely because
he knew that poverty was not the result of individual fecklessness
or slothfulness, but was often the result of greed and manipulation
by those who wield economic and political power. As Mesters has
observed, such a reading of Jesus' words subverts the kind of interpretation offered by sophisticated exegetes in the First World:

> Before the movement of renewal through the basic communities
> began, the Bible was always on the side of those who teach,
> give orders, and hand out pay, and it was explained in a way
> that confirmed the knowledge of those who taught, the power of
> those who gave orders, and the wealth of those who paid. Now
> the Bible is beginning to be on the side of those who are taught,
> ordered and paid, and these people are discovering exactly the
> opposite of what was always considered the teaching confirmed
> by the Bible. (1989: 7)

Just as the socio-economic background of interpreters may have
influenced their exegesis of a biblical text, so their theological convictions and religious affiliations may have exerted an influence on
their biblical interpretation. In this regard, we may take our example from the Old Testament and, in particular, the way in which the
history of Israel is represented in much recent scholarship. Garbini,
who conveniently provides a valuable overview of various recent
attempts to write a 'History of Israel', is deeply critical of those 'for
whom an unacknowledged confessional interest . . . appears to have
predominated over a concern for scientific objectivity' (1988: 55). In
a similar vein, Philip Davies accuses scholars who have engaged in
writing a 'History of Israel' of having been 'motivated by theology
and religious sentiment, not critical scholarship'.[19] He argues that
their religious commitments have led ineluctably to a bias in favour
of the biblical text as historically reliable; consequently, they have
tended to adopt the perspective of the biblical text and allowed it
to assume a position of unquestioned priority in their reconstructions of Israel's history. The result of such an ideological bias is that
the standard 'Histories of Israel' differ little from one another in
their presentation of the material, for their authors merely repeat
or paraphrase the biblical text, supplementing it occasionally with

alleged parallels from documents elsewhere in the ancient Near East.[20] The confessional approach adopted by such scholars has meant that instead of studying the biblical material with the necessary detachment they have perpetuated the bias of the biblical sources and accepted unquestioningly the perspective of the biblical authors.[21] For example, instead of forming their own unprejudiced opinion about the moral compass of the Canaanites, they have simply repeated the biblical 'line' that these people were basically immoral, evil and debauched.[22] Davies argues that such scholars have failed to step outside the ideology of the text, and their presuppositions about the central significance and authority of the Bible have prevented them from engaging in real historical research. According to Davies, only when the Old Testament is viewed as a cultural artefact rather than a document of faith can adequate conclusions be made regarding the reliability of the biblical account.

In response to such criticisms of scholarly endeavours, Iain Provan has argued that the secular, anti-theological stance of scholars such as Philip Davies is no less ideological than those of the approaches which he so vehemently attacks. Indeed, Provan criticizes Davies and other like-minded scholars for highlighting the ideology of others while carefully concealing their own: 'the noisy ejection of religious commitment through the *front* door of the scholarly house is only a cover for the quieter smuggling in (whether conscious or unconscious) of a quite different form of commitment through the *rear*' (1995: 605). The difference between Davies and the scholars whom he opposes is that he seems to be blithely unaware of his own ideological presuppositions: 'The real division in scholarship is, of course, not between those who have a philosophical system and those who do not. It is between those who realise that they have one and those who are innocent of the fact' (591 n.27).

The arguments regarding the extent to which ideology has influenced the presentation of Israel's history in the Old Testament will no doubt continue, but it seems clear that the biblical authors were not disinterested bystanders of the events that they purported to record; rather, they had an argument to advance, a case to put, an agenda to promote. They were, in the words of David Clines, 'interested parties' (1995) and this is something that must surely be factored in to any future discussion of the 'history of Israel' as reflected in the Bible.

Conclusion

Ideological criticism is charged with the difficult task of making the ideological opacities of the biblical text transparent, for the text often conceals more than it reveals, and even the most seemingly neutral narratives are often laced with particular values and presuppositions that may not be particularly evident on a superficial reading of the text. Moreover, since the Bible is the product of many authors and editors, it is only to be expected that it contains a concatenation of many distinct voices and viewpoints; certainly, too many interests are represented and too many factions have influenced the material to enable us to say that the Bible represents a single, uniform ideological viewpoint. For this reason, it is incumbent upon the biblical scholar to ask some searching questions. From whose perspective is a particular narrative related? Whose class, gender or ethnic interests are being served by a particular text? Whose voice is being privileged and whose voice is being marginalized, suppressed or excluded? The answer to such questions may help us to identify the group that brought the text into existence and was instrumental in preserving it.

But ideological criticism is concerned not only with a systematic study of the ideology inscribed in the biblical text but also with the ideological position embraced (whether consciously or not) by the biblical interpreter, for it is argued that the ideological baggage of the scholar may well influence the results of his or her exegesis. Readers are thus encouraged to recognize their own ideological involvement with the text, and to consider how their own socio-cultural and economic background may determine not only *how* they read a particular text but also *which* text they decide to read. Ideological criticism therefore challenges readers to reflect critically upon their own assumptions and to explore as openly and honestly as they can their own interpretative interests.

As was noted at the beginning of this chapter, the very word 'ideology' was scarcely mentioned in scholarly discussions of the Bible just four decades ago. By now, however, ideology has emerged as an issue of major importance in biblical scholarship and has rightly taken its place alongside reader-response criticism, feminist criticism and postcolonial criticism as a legitimate area of scholarly inquiry. Some will no doubt question whether the subject really merits the considerable attention recently lavished upon it by biblical scholars, but the fact is that it has proved helpful in drawing attention not only to the social and political aspects of biblical thought but also to the unconscious prejudices and presuppositions of those who read and interpret the Bible.

CHAPTER FOUR

Postcolonial criticism

When the white man came to our country, he had the Bible and we had the land. The white man said to us, 'Let us pray'. After the prayer, the white man had the land and we had the Bible.

A popular South African saying

John-Paul II, we, Andean and American Indians, have decided to take advantage of your visit to return to you your Bible, since in five centuries it has not given us love, peace or justice. Please take back your Bible and give it back to our oppressors, because they need its moral teachings more than we do. Ever since the arrival of Christopher Columbus, a culture, a language, religion and values which belong to Europe have been imposed on Latin America by force.

An open letter to Pope John-Paul II on his visit to Peru
from various indigenous movements

[T]here is abundant evidence, especially in traditions of imperialist colonialism emanating from so-called Christian countries, for appeal to sacred writings to justify inhumane behaviour.

Michael Prior

It is a characteristic weakness of biblical exegesis in the modern Western tradition . . . that although it has dignified itself with the rhetoric of objectivity, it has frequently been blind to its own cultural assumptions.

Mark G. Brett

As a method of inquiry postcolonial theory occurs in a variety of academic subjects, including anthropology, sociology, history,

English literature and cultural studies, and although its application varies from one discipline to another its basic aim is the same,
namely, to uncover colonial domination in all its forms and oppose
imperial assumptions and ideologies.[1] As a critical theory its entry
into the arena of biblical studies is comparatively late, for it was not
until the 1990s that scholars in the Third World and those among
racial minorities in the US began to raise questions about the role
of the Bible in the imperial cause and the extent to which colonial
assumptions are embedded in the text.[2] One of the main aims of
postcolonial criticism is to read the Bible from the perspective of
the socially excluded and oppressed, and to expose and oppose
texts that appear to condone various forms of tyranny, domination
and abuse.

The present chapter examines the extent to which the Bible has
been implicated in colonial rule, and it will consider how it was
appropriated both by the colonizer to justify oppression and by the
colonized to articulate their identity and self-worth. Imperialism
is, of course, an ancient concept, and so its pervasive presence in
the Bible is hardly surprising. Since both the Old Testament and
the New emerged within a landscape of imperial domination and
control, it will be necessary to examine the impact that successive empires – Egyptian, Assyrian, Babylonian, Persian, Hellenistic
and Roman – had upon the people of ancient Israel and the nascent Christian movement. But postcolonial criticism is concerned
to examine imperial impulses not only within the biblical text but
also within biblical interpretation; thus it will be necessary to consider how interpretations of the Bible by those who have experienced the legacy of colonization have challenged and undermined
the interpretative authority of scholars in the West.

Colonial rule and the Bible

From the fifteenth through to the eighteenth centuries, Western
Europe engaged in a programme of territorial expansion and
began to extend its sphere of influence across the world. By the
start of the nineteenth century, it is estimated that Europe had colonized 35 per cent of the non-European world, and by the beginning of the First World War this had increased to 85 per cent (Said
1978: 39–41). The process of colonization was based on a firm
belief in European superiority and in an unassailable conviction

that civilization was destined to advance over barbarism. Colonial propaganda instilled in the natives the belief that the ruler knew better than the ruled, and that whatever the colonial master did, however unpleasant or unpalatable, was ultimately for the benefit of the subject people. Emphasis was placed on the native-friendly, sympathetic and benevolent face of colonialism, for its aim was merely to bring law and order to unruly people and abolish practices – such as witchcraft and ritual sacrifice – which the civilized world had long outgrown. Any perceived violence on the part of the colonizers was simply the inevitable consequence of their attempt to put an end to savagery and internecine tribal warfare. The imperial masters, convinced that their incursions into foreign lands were ultimately for the benefit of the indigenous population, could thus exercise political rule with a clear conscience. After all, what was wrong with ridding the world of polygamy and human sacrifice? What harm could there be in delivering the natives from the twin evils of ignorance and savagery, and replacing them with the benefits of education and civilized values? What was wrong with helping the indigenous population to renounce their corrupt and superstitious practices and encouraging them to embrace, instead, the enlightened ethos and progressive values of the West? Surely orderliness and democracy were preferable to the chaos and anarchy that had existed prior to colonial rule? Far from being an aggressive imposition of one culture upon another, the colonial enterprise was a well-meaning and benevolent intrusion into the lives of the natives, and the subject people should be grateful for such generous and charitable intervention, for there was little doubt that, were the colonizers to leave, the natives would simply revert to their old, barbaric ways.

At the beginning of the British Empire's colonizing programme, the Bible itself played a relatively insignificant part in the process of establishing political domination over the natives; its circulation and availability were fairly limited and its impact was therefore quite minimal. It was not until much later that the Bible began to be used to undergird the imperial designs of the colonizer (see Sugirtharajah 2001: 45–73). That development came about, at least in part, as a result of the British and Foreign Bible Society's concerted effort to make the Bible more easily readable and affordable to ordinary people, irrespective of their social condition or economic status.[3] But once the Bible was given to the colonized, it soon became an instrument of domination, which could be used to promote social structures that perpetuated an unjust and oppressive system.[4] The distinction between master and servant, governor and governed, rich and poor, was something that had been authorized and sanctioned by Scripture itself (see Rom. 13.1–10). After all, the slave-based society was something that was presupposed in the Bible and was an institution that existed not only in ancient Israel but also in the period of the Early Church. The Bible taught that everyone had a divinely given status in life, and that the status of the black indigenous population was to be subservient to their white European counterparts who had been ordained by God to be the superior race. Colonialism was based on an overweening desire for power and domination, and the Bible provided the very ammunition that the colonizers needed to achieve their aim. Thus, like other literary works, such as Homer's *Iliad*, the Bible came to function as an 'imperializing text', for it served to authorize expansionist activities and legitimate imperializing agendas.[5] Of course, that the Bible should be used in this way was highly ironic, given that the biblical traditions were produced by people who were themselves frequently subjected to imperial domination.

While some among the colonized were taken in by the ideology of those in positions of power, and even expressed gratitude and admiration towards the colonizer, others cast doubt on their supposed altruistic motives, and were by no means convinced that colonization was the benevolent humanitarian enterprise that the colonizer would have them believe. The kind of propaganda disseminated by the colonizers – that the natives were basically barbarous people who were quite incapable of ruling themselves – came to be regarded as patronizing in the extreme and smacked of cultural arrogance. While apologists for the colonial programme regarded it as a positive development and claimed that there was nothing wrong with regenerating and civilizing people who were living in darkness, those at the receiving end of such supposed blessings were aware of the predatory, exploitative nature of colonial rule and its various strategies of domination. For them, the atrocities committed in the name of empire – including land-seizures, forced resettlements and economic exploitation – merely highlighted the rapacious nature of the colonial enterprise. They viewed the colonizers as a culturally disruptive force, intent upon imposing their own economic system and political rule on foreign nations, so that the natives virtually felt themselves to be strangers in their own

land. The values of the indigenous population had to be accommodated to those of the colonizer, who were determined to suppress
cultural diversity and promote, instead, a few universal standards
for the benefit of those in positions of power.

Such resentment inevitably led to a rebellion against the colonial
masters, and the Bible, which had been used as such an effective tool
to keep the subject people firmly in place, now came to be used as
an equally effective instrument to shape the resistance to colonization. Instead of being hapless consumers of imperial interpretations
of the Bible, the colonized began to claim the authority to interpret
Scripture from their own perspective, and when Scripture was read
by those who had suffered repression, persecution and exclusion, its
message came to be understood very differently. Contrary to what
the colonial missionaries had preached, the Bible did not provide
comforting answers to the problems of human despair and suffering.
As Sarojini Nadar has observed, the kind of argument produced by
Job's companions ('Has any innocent person ever perished? Where
have the upright ever been destroyed?'; Job 4.7) made as little sense
to the inhabitants of countries devastated by the insidious effects
of colonization as it did to Job himself (2006: 195). The colonized
came to the Bible from a context of oppression and disenfranchise-
ment, and they realized that the very book which had been used to
legitimate social and economic injustice, could equally well be used
to liberate them from oppressive and cruel regimes. Texts that had
been cited to promote an attitude of resignation and apathy in the
face of exploitation could just as well be used to foment rebellion
and to revitalize the life and culture of the indigenous people. The
colonized had discovered the revolutionary potential of the Bible
and realized that, instead of being an instrument of oppression, it
could become a vehicle of emancipation, and that they themselves
could become empowered, rather than subjugated, by the words
of Scripture. Of course, the colonized had no theological training
or exegetical expertise, but, for them, that hardly mattered; what
was important was that the Bible spoke meaningfully to their own
experience of struggle and oppression, and that it was possible to
extract from an ancient text a message that was relevant to their
own situation. For the colonized, the purpose of Bible study was not
to glean information about the past but to illuminate and inform
the present, and by reading the text in this way they were able to
discover a new self-identity and self-worth.

It is clear, then, that there were two opposing views regarding the programme of colonization: while the colonized focussed on the evils of imperial rule, the colonizers emphasized its virtues and indispensability. Moreover, in the colonial context, the Bible functioned as something of a two-edged sword: for the colonizer it was a convenient instrument of oppression and subjugation, while for the colonized it became a means to reassert their own identity and culture.[6] Before examining in more detail some of the biblical texts appropriated by the colonizer and the colonized, it may be useful to consider two familiar passages, one from the Old Testament and one from the New, in order to appreciate how such texts might be interpreted by scholars from the former colonies. In the first text, Laura E. Donaldson reads the story of the book of Ruth from the perspective of a Cherokee woman, and highlights the often neglected role of Orpah in the narrative. In the second, Musa Dube, from Botswana, examines the story of Jesus' encounter with the woman of Samaria in John 4, and brings to prominence its hidden imperialist agenda.

Two postcolonial readings

The book of Ruth relates how a man named Elimelech, along with his wife, Naomi, and their two sons, decided to leave their home in Judah because of the famine in the land, and settle down in Moab. While there, the two sons married Moabite women, Orpah and Ruth. Elimelech died and, some years later, both his sons also died, leaving behind Naomi, the widow, and her two daughters-in-law. When Naomi heard that there was no longer a famine in Judah, she decided to return to her homeland and, accompanied by Ruth and Orpah, they began on their journey. At one point, Naomi, realizing that her daughters-in-law may prefer to remain in their own country, encouraged them to return: 'Go back, both of you, home to your own mothers' (Ruth 1.8). Initially, the two women insisted on accompanying their mother-in-law (1.10), but after further encouragement from Naomi, Orpah took her leave and returned to Moab, leaving Ruth and Naomi to make the journey together to Judah.

Laura Donaldson begins her study of the story by focussing on Moab, the place in which Elimelech and his family had settled.

According to the biblical tradition, Moab was the home of a 'sexually promiscuous and scandalous' population (1999: 23). The Israelites regarded the women of Moab, in particular, as agents of impurity and evil (see Num. 25.1–5), and Deut. 23.3 expressly states that no Moabite would be accepted as members of the community of Israel, even to the tenth generation. Thus by deciding to leave behind the wicked and evil country of her upbringing, and accompanying Naomi to Judah, Ruth was making a deliberate choice to renounce her own depraved and degenerate culture and embrace, instead, the superior culture of the Jews. As befitted the woman who was to become the direct ancestress of King David (Ruth 4.13–17), she was prepared to sacrifice her home, her kindred and her native religion and become a God-fearing Jewess. Not surprisingly, the later rabbis regarded her in a favourable light, seeing her as the paradigmatic convert to Judaism. Indeed, her faith was regarded as greater even than that of Abraham, for she left her home of her own volition, whereas the patriarch left Ur only in response to God's command.

Donaldson points out that Ruth's decision to accompany her mother-in-law instead of returning to her homeland would not be regarded in such a positive light by American Indians, for they see it as a story of a woman who forsakes her own people and aligns herself with the very nation that was instructed to destroy the religious heritage of her enemies (Deut. 12.2–3). Ruth's decision to renounce her own ethnic and cultural identity and assimilate herself to a foreign way of life would be regarded by them as a kind of betrayal of her indigenous heritage. Orpah, on the other hand, is viewed in a much more positive light, for she had no desire to turn her back on her own ancestral traditions, nor was she willing to go to a land ruled by a deity other than the one that she had traditionally worshipped. When the book of Ruth is read from the cultural and historical perspective of an American-Indian woman, Ruth's action serves to symbolize the inevitable vanishing of the indigenes' culture, while Orpah's decision symbolizes the refusal of minority cultures to become assimilated to their 'civilized' white counterparts.

Clearly, Donaldson's reading of the book of Ruth subverts the traditional interpretation of the narrative, for it 'transforms Ruth's positive value into a negative and Orpah's negative value into a positive', and she ends her article by expressing the hope that she has provided an interpretation 'that resists imperial exegesis and contributes to the empowerment of aboriginal peoples everywhere' (1999: 36).

Turning to the encounter between Jesus and the woman of Samaria in John 4, Musa Dube has sought to locate the passage in its imperial setting and consider the ways in which the Johannine text may be viewed as colluding with the project of colonization. The story is significant since it may be classed as a 'mission narrative', which embraces the ideology of expansion, as Jesus' mission begins to extend its influence as far as Samaria. The author of the narrative[7] contrives to conceal the missionary aspect of the Jesus movement by implying that Jesus was merely in transit through Samaria on his way to Galilee (vv. 3–4); there was no intention of entering the region and embarking on a missionary programme, for Jesus merely rested by a well because he was tired (v. 6) and it is the Samaritans themselves who ask him to stay (v. 40). Meanwhile, the disciples go into the city, but the purpose of their journey was to buy food, not to embark on a mission (v. 8). The Samaritans' declaration that 'Jesus is the Saviour of the world' (v. 42) shows the Johannine Jesus emerging 'fully clothed in the emperor's titles' (2006: 307) and his superior status is indicated by the fact that he is greater than Jacob (v. 12) and is not merely a prophet (v. 19) but the Messiah (vv. 25–6). Just as colonizers typically berate the natives, condemning their pagan religious practices and casting aspersions on their moral life, so in this story the Samaritans are portrayed as ignorant ('You Samaritans worship what you do not know'; v. 22), and the Samaritan woman herself is depicted as lacking in moral scruples ('You have had five husbands and the man with whom you are now living is not your husband'; v. 18). By contrast, Jesus appears as all-knowing (vv. 10, 22, 39) and powerful (vv. 14, 42); he is able to teach the community and offer answers to the questions posed by the people (vv. 21–6). Significantly, it is in this story that Jesus claims that the fields are 'ripe for harvesting' (v. 35). The story is about the gospel making forays into the gentile world, and, by implication, into the pagan world, which, in colonial terms, means evangelizing Asia, Africa and Latin America. Thus, viewed from the perspective of the colonized, this is a story 'that authorizes Christian disciples/readers/believers to travel, enter, educate and to harvest other foreign lands for the Christian nations' (307).

Such interpretations of familiar biblical texts show how the Bible is read very differently by exploited peoples and marginalized cultures. Of course, such analyses of the biblical text tend to unsettle mainstream conclusions; nevertheless, they bring a fresh approach to the Bible brought about by a new context of reading and the radically different cultural-political location of the reader. The importance of such readings is that they provide oppositional voices which undermine and transform mainstream, white, Western interpretations of the text. In doing so, postcolonial critics have thrown down the gauntlet and challenged the traditional context and practices of Western biblical scholarship.

The use of the Bible by the colonizer

There was no shortage of passages in the Bible, which appeared to justify colonial rule. Three biblical texts from the book of Genesis proved particularly amenable to the early colonizers. First, the divine command in Gen. 1.28 to 'fill the earth and subdue it' was often cited, from the sixteenth century onwards, as a biblical justification for colonial expansion. These words were understood by the colonizers as a warrant for violence and domination, and were taken to mean that God himself had ordained that one culture – the culture of the colonizer – should claim superiority over all others, extending its influence over the face of the earth for the mutual benefit of human kind (see Brett 2008: 32–9). The second text, Gen. 28.14 ('you shall spread abroad to the west and to the east and to the north and to the south') was believed to contain a prophecy which saw its fulfilment in the expansion of British colonial rule to the four corners of the earth during the sixteenth to the nineteenth centuries.

The third text, in Gen. 9.18–27, requires more detailed discussion, for this passage, long regarded as morally problematic by biblical scholars, recounts the so-called curse of Ham. The story relates how Ham saw the nakedness of his father, Noah, but instead of covering him up immediately he merely reported his father's condition to his two brothers, Shem and Japheth. They, in turn, displayed proper respect for their father by covering his nakedness, and when Noah woke up he pronounced a curse on Ham but blessed his brothers for showing proper paternal respect.

Although the words of the curse refer to Canaan, it is clear that the same person who committed the outrage in v. 22 is the one who is cursed in vv. 25–7: 'Cursed be Canaan! Most servile of slaves shall he be to his brothers . . . bless, O LORD, the tents of Shem; may Canaan be his slave. May God extend Japheth's boundaries, let him dwell in the tents of Shem, may Canaan be his slave'.[8] All the descendants of Ham/Canaan were regarded as having been implicated in the curse, and according to the table of nations in Gen. 10.6–14 these descendants included the Cushites, the Egyptians and the Phutites, people whose countries were located on the continent of Africa. The curse in Genesis meant that Ham/Canaan and his descendants were destined to become slaves, and the early rabbis took this to refer to a universal curse on black people.[9] In the fifth-century Midrash, Noah is represented as saying to Ham, 'You have prevented me from doing something in the dark, therefore your seed will be ugly and dark-skinned' (*Midrash Bereshith Rabbah* 1.293), and the sixth-century Babylonian Talmud states that 'the descendants of Ham are cursed by being black and are sinful with degenerate progeny' (see Felder 1991a: 132). This negative stereotyping of black people continued into the Middle Ages, and the early colonizers regarded the curse of Ham as sanctioning the enslavement of Africans and as a sign that their subordinate status had been preordained by God.

Of all the biblical texts that were appealed to by the early colonizers, however, the most potent was undoubtedly the story of the conquest of Canaan as recorded in the book of Joshua.[10] According to the biblical account, the Israelites, as God's 'chosen people', were given a divine command to enter the land of Canaan, annihilate the native population and settle in the land themselves, distributing it between the various tribes.[11] The European colonizers found in these narratives material to justify their invasion of America, just as the ancient Israelites, in accordance with God's decree, had invaded Canaan. Moreover, the idea propagated in the Old Testament of Israel as the 'chosen people' set much of the tone for the shaping of colonial power and influence. In the late seventeenth century, the Puritans who settled in New England regarded themselves as God's 'elect' who were embarking on a new exodus with a divine mandate to confront the indigenous population with an Israelite 'right of conquest'.[12] They even identified the Native Americans with the idolatrous Canaanites and Amalekites of old – people who, if they would not be converted, were surely worthy of annihilation.[13] The colonized were depicted as morally and spiritually degenerate and in need of salvation, and their unbelief, idolatry and abominations amply justified the appropriation of their land – land that the natives were quite unworthy to occupy. The divine mandate to conquer the indigenous population of Canaan was similarly used to support Western colonizing enterprises in Latin America and South Africa, which resulted in the untold suffering of millions of people (see Mosala 1993: 63).

In addition to such passages from the Old Testament, there was much material in the New Testament which could be used to defend imperial ideology and sustain the colonial mission. Inevitably, one of the most significant passages was Jesus' statement concerning the payment of taxes to Caesar (Mk 12.13–7). In response to the question posed to him by the Pharisees and the Herodians as to whether it was lawful to pay tribute to the emperor, Jesus replied: 'Pay Caesar what belongs to Caesar and to God what belongs to God' (v. 17). It is easy to see how these words were used by the colonizers to defend their pro-imperialist agenda, for Jesus was here clearly using the language of compliance with regard to the emperor and was encouraging an attitude of subordination to the state. Jesus, having been afforded a golden opportunity to deny the legitimacy of the Roman imperial power in Palestine, refused to do so and, instead, appeared to recognize Roman sovereignty and favour the continuation of the status quo. Further, Jesus' so-called Great Mission command ('Go, therefore, to all nations and make them my disciples . . . and teach them to observe all that I have commanded you'; Mt. 28.19–20) similarly played into the hands of the colonial rulers, for it was interpreted to provide biblical legitimacy for missionary expansion into Asia, Africa and Latin America.[14]

Paul's missionary journeys as depicted in such passages as Acts 13–14; 15.40–18.23; 18.24–21.14 were also regarded as important texts during territorial expansion by European nations, for they provided further Scriptural sanction for the colonial enterprise (see Sugirtharajah 1998: 91–116). Luke's narrative of the Gentile mission shows Paul conforming closely to the Roman imperial order; indeed, the apostle seems to enjoy a positive relationship with the Roman officials: when accused of a crime he could confidently appeal to the emperor to settle the case (Acts 25.11), and it was the Roman military that intervened to rescue him from murderous plots by his fellow Jews (see Kahl 2008: 137–56). Further, Paul's own attitude to the state in such passages as Rom. 13.1–7 seems overwhelmingly positive, for here he clearly endorses the authority of the Roman empire and encourages his followers to show deference to those who ruled over them: 'Every person must submit to the authorities in power' (v. 1). Those who avoided wrongdoing had nothing to fear from the governing authorities, for they were merely 'God's agents working for your own good' (v. 4).

Finally, the Bible proved a useful weapon in the colonial defence of slavery, for it appeared to sanction, or at least tolerate, the institution. Appeal was made to the laws of the Old Testament, which regulated slavery (see Ex. 21.1–11, 26–7), and it was argued that what was regulated by law was, by definition, not forbidden, but sanctioned. Moreover, neither Jesus nor Paul spoke a word against slavery and neither made any attempt to eradicate the custom. Indeed, quite the contrary, for Paul requests Philemon to take Onesimus, the fugitive slave, back in his former state of servitude, and gives as his reason for doing so the master's right to the service of his slave (Philemon 8–20). Paul's pronouncements in 1 Cor. 7.20–4 provided further support for the cause of the slave owners, for the apostle seems to exhort slaves to accept placidly their status in life: 'Everyone is to remain before God in the condition in which he received his call' (v. 24). Moreover, the so-called Household Codes encountered in some of the Deutero-Pauline epistles (e.g. Col. 3.18–4.1; Ephes. 5.21–6.9) reinforce the hierarchical ordering of society by demanding conformity to generally accepted societal norms.[15]

It is clear from the above selection of texts favoured by the colonizer that the Bible was being used to legitimate, consolidate and promote the dominant values and ideological interests of the ruling classes. As we shall see, however, when biblical texts are read from the margins rather than through the lens of the custodians of political power, a very different picture emerges.

The use of the Bible by the colonized

As might be expected, the colonized took issue with the kind of interpretation of the Bible outlined above. They realized, to begin with, that the colonizers had been very selective in their choice of texts, for they had conveniently by-passed biblical passages that may have undermined or threatened their imperial ambitions. Did not the prophets challenge the gross abuses of power by the monarchy and the ostentatious greed of the prosperous merchants and landowners? Did not the law legislate against all kinds of socioeconomic injustice? Did not the Psalmist and the authors of the Wisdom literature condemn those who were indifferent to, or complicit in, the oppressive systems of their day? Moreover, the colonized regarded it as part of their remit to rectify colonial misinterpretations of the Bible and expose the way in which biblical texts had been used by the colonizers to serve their own purpose. It was observed, for example, that, in the broader context of Gen. 1–11, the divine command to 'subdue the earth' (Gen. 1.28) was more a matter of caring for its resources that subduing it; indeed, the Tower of Babel story in Gen. 11 was designed as a clear warning that any attempt to claim the cultural high ground was contrary to God's will. As Mark G. Brett has rightly observed, the 'hermeneutical hubris' of the early colonizers 'actually inverted the communicative intentions of the biblical primeval narratives as we now have them' (2008: 2). Moreover, their interpretation of the Ham episode in Gen. 9 merely demonstrated how the influence of early rabbinic readings of the text came to take precedence over what the text itself actually said, and provided a classic example of how a biblical passage could be misused and misappropriated in support of a particular cause.

The same was true of the use made by the colonizers of the exodus-conquest account in the book of Joshua, for postcolonial criticism was able to demonstrate that texts that were liberating in one context may well be oppressive in another. How different would the narrative appear if the Canaanites, rather than the Israelites, were placed at the centre of theological reflection? It was precisely from the Canaanites' perspective that the narrative was viewed by the Australian Aborigines, the New Zealand Maoris, the Native Americans and the Palestinians, for, like the indigenous population of Canaan, they, too, had been faced with disruption and dispersion in their own lands.[16] In this regard, postcolonial critics took issue with liberation theologians, who had appropriated the story of the exodus and conquest in their long and tortuous struggle against colonialism, imperialism and dictatorship. They had viewed the narrative as reflecting the common experience of suffering, and the exodus from Egypt was seen as a symbol of throwing off the yoke and breaking free from established institutions, enabling people who had been marginalized and oppressed to refashion a new life for themselves. Moses' words to Pharaoh, 'Let my people go!' had a particular resonance for the poor and powerless, and the story of Israel's release from bondage provided a beacon of hope for all who were in despair. But the problem with such an interpretation, according to the postcolonial critics, was that it did not consider the plight of the victims who were at the receiving end of God's liberating action. Liberation theologians, such as Gustavo Gutiérrez, had read these narratives uncritically, without any awareness of, or sensitivity to, the plight of the Canaanites.[17] Gutiérrez referred to the oppression suffered by the Hebrews in the 'land of slavery' (Ex. 13.3; 20.2) and emphasized their repression (Ex. 1.11) and humiliation (Ex. 1.13–14), but said nothing about the oppression and humiliation suffered by the indigenous population of Canaan at the hands of those very slaves. He claimed that the liberation of Israel was 'the beginning of the construction of a just and comradely society' (1974: 88). But a 'just and comradely society' for whom? Certainly not for the Canaanites, who, according to the biblical tradition, were annihilated by the invading Israelites. This one-sided emphasis on the liberating agenda of the Old Testament had led liberation theologians to overlook – or perhaps deliberately ignore – its oppressive aspects. To extol freedom was perfectly laudable, but when that freedom was achieved at the expense of others it became problematic. As Michael Prior has correctly observed, if the exodus theme had been combined with the conquest theme we would have been left not with 'a paradigm for liberation, but for colonial plunder'.[18]

Turning to the New Testament, postcolonial criticism was again able to highlight the one-sided and selective approach adopted by the colonizers. Jesus' enigmatic reply concerning the payment of tribute to Caesar did not imply a wholehearted approval on his part of the Roman Empire's system of taxation; his point was simply that the imposition of taxes on subject nations was quite unlike the rule of God. There can be little doubt that Jesus saw Roman rule as oppressive, as his critical remarks about the kings of the Gentiles clearly indicate: 'You know that among the Gentiles the recognized rulers lord it over their subjects, and the great make their authority felt' (Mk 10.42). While earthly rulers wield authority over the poor and exploit them to their own advantage, 'it shall not be so among you' (Mk 10.43). Jesus' followers would have understood him to be challenging the conventional constructions of power symbolized by Roman imperial rule. The kingdom that Jesus proclaimed was far removed from the tyrannical jurisdiction exercised by the empires of this world, and its appearance would herald a complete change in the present regime. His command to his followers to feed the hungry, house the homeless, clothe the naked and comfort the afflicted (Mt. 25.31–46) stood in sharp contrast to the dominant imperial patterns of government. Moreover, Jesus took the side of the oppressed against the officially constituted religious and political authorities, and he condemned the rich for their abuse of power and spoke out against injustice and exploitation in all its forms. Indeed, his general teaching was completely at odds with imperial ideals and values: 'whoever wants to be great must be your servant, and whoever wants to be first must be the slave of all' (Mk 10.43–4). That Jesus was regarded as a threat to the imperial order is clear from the fact that he was crucified as an insurgent leader, and it is not without significance that the inscription on the cross mockingly proclaimed him to be the 'king of the Jews' (Mt. 27.37). The fact that Jesus' followers, after his crucifixion, bestowed upon him the titles 'Lord', 'redeemer', 'saviour', 'Son of God' – titles that were used of Caesar even before Jesus' time – indicates that they insisted on loyalty to Jesus as opposed to the Roman emperor.

Further, the argument that the institution of slavery could be justified on biblical grounds was regarded as disingenuous, for although the Old Testament sanctioned slavery, it also sanctioned many other customs – such as blood vengeance – which clearly were no longer binding. Moreover, the colonized were not slow to point out that a certain irony existed in the fact that, according to the biblical tradition, no sooner had the Hebrew slaves escaped from servitude in Egypt than they promulgated laws which effectively sanctioned the institution! As Kirk-Duggan caustically remarked, 'slavery was bad for them to experience but acceptable for them to initiate and practice' (2006: 260). Nor was the appeal to the New Testament any more persuasive. Those who argued that Paul placed his seal of approval on the institution of slavery had conveniently failed to observe that elsewhere the apostle's teaching suggested that he favoured a more equitable social system. In 1 Cor. 12.13,

Paul states that 'we were all brought into one body by baptism, whether Jews or Greeks, slaves or free', a sentiment repeated in Gal. 3.28, where the apostle claims that there is 'no such thing as Jew and Greek, slave and free, male and female; for you are all one person in Christ Jesus'. The apostle's statement in 1 Cor. 7.24 had been completely misinterpreted by the colonizers, for his exhortation to 'remain in the state in which you were called' was not an appeal to accept present social conditions with a pious resignation, but an encouragement to believers to remain loyal to their calling to Christ.

The appeal to Rom. 13 by the colonizers to prove that Paul endorsed the authority of the Roman state without reservation and approved of the dominant imperial order was regarded by postcolonial critics as a further example of colonizers citing selective biblical texts that happened to be congenial to the particular viewpoint which they embraced, and the particular cause that they wished to advance. Elsewhere in his letters, Paul's statements seem decidedly anti-imperial in tone. In 1 Cor. 2.6, he insists that the 'wisdom belonging to this present age or to its governing powers' was 'already in decline'. Indeed, he even suggests that the defeat of the imperial power had already begun, for Christ, enthroned in heaven, would depose 'every sovereignty, authority, and power' before delivering up the kingdom to God the Father (1 Cor. 15.24). Paul's apparent pro-imperial stance in Rom. 13 may simply have been a case of heading off even the appearance of civic unrest in a potentially volatile situation.

Finally, postcolonial critics pointed out that the colonizers steadfastly avoided any reference to the two apocalyptic writings in the Bible, namely, the book of Daniel in the Old Testament and the book of Revelation in the New. Daniel 7 contains visions in which successive empires are represented as destructive beasts, and the message is that God would execute judgement on the oppressive rulers and restore sovereignty to 'the people of the holy ones of the Most High'. The book of Revelation is uncompromising in its condemnation of the Roman Empire and undoubtedly represents the most anti-imperial of all the New Testament writings. Here, the empire is regarded as the very embodiment of destructive, demonic forces. The dramatic symbolism of Rev. 13 depicts Rome as the 'beast' that opposes God and coerces worship of the emperor (vv. 11–12), while in 17.1–6 Rome is represented by Babylon the 'whore', whose opulent lifestyle is built on violence and the destruction of human lives. In opposition to the empire's demand for their allegiance, the faithful must bear witness to Jesus, knowing that they will have to endure persecution that may even lead to martyrdom.

The above brief overview of the way the Bible has been used by the colonizer and the colonized shows how the biblical text can give legitimacy to opposing ideologies. On the one hand, it was used by those in power to justify social and economic injustices and to promote attitudes of resignation and compliance in the face of exploitation, while, on the other, it was used by the marginalized and oppressed to articulate their self-worth and empowerment. Such arguments and counter-arguments merely underline the problems that can accrue when a selective approach to the Bible is adopted. Moreover, they serve as a reminder that the Bible can be used by different groups for different purposes, and that not all uses of the Bible are for the common good.

Empire in the Bible

Postcolonial criticism regards it as part of its remit to examine representations of empire within the Bible, and to consider how colonial assumptions have informed and influenced the production of the biblical texts.[19] The Bible is a collection of ancient documents that emerged out of various colonial contexts, and the biblical texts were shaped by the social and political domination of successive empires, including Egypt, Assyria, Babylon, Persia, Greece and Rome.

According to Norman Gottwald, the people of Israel originated in a reaction against oppressive imperial regimes. 'Early Israel', he writes, 'was born as an anti-imperial resistance movement that broke away from Egyptian and Canaanite domination to become a self-governing community of free peasants' (2008: 9). Prior to the eighth century BCE, Israel and Judah had managed to retain political self-determination, and although they had to fight campaigns against neighbouring nations, there was no great empire that posed a serious threat to the people. In the third quarter of the eighth century BCE, however, this situation changed decisively when the great Assyrian empire began to flex its muscles. As John Bright has observed, 'Assyria took the path of empire in earnest, and the cloud long lowering on the horizon became a line storm which swept the little peoples before it like leaves' (2000: 269). The policy of the Assyrians was to deport the conquered peoples and incorporate their lands as provinces within the empire, and this is precisely what happened in the case of Israel. The assault under Sargon II in 724–721 BCE led to the deportation of the Israelites from their land, and this resulted in the dissolution of the northern state (2 Kgs 17).

Judah survived for another century and a half, until 597 BCE, when the Babylonian Empire laid siege to Jerusalem and replaced the government with leaders supportive of the imperial regime; in their second conquest of Judah, ten years later, Nebuchadnezzar's army destroyed Jerusalem and the temple and deported the upper echelons of society to Babylon, leaving behind a devastated land and a decimated people (2 Kgs 23). The fate of those deported to Babylon was not as miserable as might be supposed, however, for they do not seem to have endured undue hardship; indeed, they were evidently allowed to build houses and engage in agricultural activities and were able to continue some sort of community life (Jer. 29.5–6). Moreover, they were not dispersed among the local population but placed in settlements of their own (see Ezek. 3.15; Ezra 2.59), thus affording them every opportunity to preserve their national identity. But the temptation to lapse from their ancestral faith and embrace the culture of the colonizer must have been acute, and it was precisely to warn against such a relapse that the prophet known as Deutero-Isaiah emerged among the exiles. His relentless emphasis on God as creator of the world (see Is. 40.12–31; 45.11–13, 18; 48.12–16) was no doubt intended as a counter-imperial assertion, demonstrating that God was the ultimate king and sovereign, and that it was he who was in absolute control of history.

The eventual fall of Babylon came quickly and with comparative ease, and the victories gained by Cyrus, king of Persia (present day Iran) brought the whole of the Babylonian empire under his control. The Persians respected the religious sensibilities of the conquered nations, and they allowed the Jewish people a measure of freedom and local autonomy. The Persian Empire eventually gave way to the Greeks, led by Alexander the Great, and they embarked on an active policy of Hellenization (1 Mac. 1.11–15; 2 Mac. 4.10–15). When Antiochus came to occupy the throne, he showed utter contempt for the religious sensibilities of the Jews by plundering the temple and removing its sacred vessels (1 Mac. 1.20–4; 2 Mac. 5.15–21). To make matters worse, an altar to Zeus was set up in the temple, an act that was famously described in the book of Daniel as 'the abomination of desolation' (Dan. 11.31; 12.11). Antiochus suspended observance of the Sabbath and the regular Jewish sacrifices and feasts, and the Jews were forced to participate in idolatrous rites (1 Mac. 1.41–64; 2 Mac. 6.1–11). However, there was increasing resistance among the Jews to Hellenistic influence, and the books of Maccabees relate how Judas Maccabeus and his followers mounted a full-scale struggle for independence and, although hopelessly outnumbered, managed to administer a crushing defeat upon the enemy. They marched to Jerusalem, tore down the defiled altar, erecting a new one in its place, and rededicated the temple with feasting and great joy. The Jews have celebrated the Feast of Hanukkah (Dedication) ever since in commemoration of this momentous event.

By New Testament times Palestine was subject to the dictates of the Roman Empire, which demanded absolute loyalty from its subjects and expected them to worship the Roman emperor and the traditional gods of Rome. Many Christians in the Early Church resisted such demands, aware of the evils that were deeply rooted in the entire system of Roman Imperial power. The book of Revelation calls for faithful endurance of persecution by the forces of empire, recognizing that it may well lead to martyrdom.

It is clear that, over the centuries, imperial rule had far-reaching repercussions which affected every aspect of the lives of the people of Israel and Judah. For example, when the Assyrian empire conquered Israel and Judah, the state demanded tribute to fund the lavish lifestyle of the ruling classes. The harsh annual exactions meant that the impoverished peasants had to take out a loan provided by mendacious money-lenders, often at staggering rates of interest,[20] and the debtors had to pay back the value of the loan out of the following harvest. When those harvests failed, as they often did, owing to drought, floods and the ravages of war, the poor peasants would be unable to repay the loan and would often lose their land and be reduced to a position of servitude.

Of course, the process of imperialization often generates a movement of resistance, and this may be seen quite clearly in both the

Old Testament and the New. Prophets such as Isaiah, for example, claimed that the great empire of Assyria was not an autonomous agent but merely a rod in the hand of Yahweh for the punishment of his people; the time would come when Assyria, too, would be punished for its ostentatious display of imperial arrogance: 'Shall the axe vaunt itself over the one who wields it, or the saw magnify itself against the one who handles it?' (Is. 10.15). The message of the prophet was perfectly clear: Assyria, the great imperial power, would be called to account and merited imminent punishment and destruction.[21] A similar message pertains to the Roman Empire in the book of Revelation: Rome's single-minded pursuit of her own power and economic advantage would be punished by God, and she would be treated as ignominiously as she had treated her subjects: 'Render to her as she herself has rendered, and repay her double for her deeds . . . as she glorified herself and lived luxuriously, so give her a like measure of torment and grief' (Rev. 18.6–7).

It is important to realize that the biblical books are not unambiguously and unanimously pro- or anti-imperial rule, for, as we have seen, the policy of various emperors towards their subjects varied enormously. While the policy of the Assyrians was to deport the people of Israel and scatter them among the nations, assimilating them into the larger empire so that their individual identity was lost, the Persians were much more accommodating to the people under their jurisdiction. Cyrus, the king of Persia, not only decreed that the Jews who had been exiled to Babylon should be permitted to return to their homeland, but he even contributed to the expense of rebuilding the temple in Jerusalem by providing funds from the royal treasury (Ezra 1.2–4). Instead of obliterating the national identity of subject peoples, as the Assyrians had done, Cyrus' policy was to allow them as far as possible to enjoy cultural autonomy within the framework of the empire and to entrust responsibility for controlling the people to native princes. Thus, while Isaiah castigates Assyria as the rod of God's anger, Deutero-Isaiah refers to Cyrus as God's 'shepherd', and the prophet even has Yahweh referring to him as his 'anointed' (Is. 44.28; 45.1).

Much work remains to be done to examine how colonialism and empire have been presented in the Bible and the influence that imperialism has had on the way in which the books of the Bible were formed. Such a study would inevitably raise a raft of questions and issues that cannot be dealt with in the present volume. How far did imperial rule shape and influence Jewish culture and customs? To what extent did the people of Israel oppose the culture of the colonizer and to what extent did they embrace it? What impact did colonialism have on gender relations and women's role within the community of the Early Church? Such issues will no doubt engage the interest of biblical scholars for many years to come.

Postcolonialism and biblical scholarship

It is part of the remit of postcolonial criticism to scrutinize and expose not only the colonial assumptions of the biblical text but also the colonial assumptions of the biblical interpreter. The two tasks are not unrelated, for the colonial impulses within the Bible have led, albeit perhaps subconsciously, to an exegetical imperialism that has often characterized biblical scholarship. Halvor Moxnes, for example, has shown how factors such as colonialism and ethnicity influenced German scholars in the nineteenth and early twentieth centuries, for they tended to inject their own cultural and racist biases into their interpretation of the biblical text. Scholars such as D. F. Strauss and E. Renan regarded the biblical world virtually as an extension of Europe, and Galilee was viewed almost as 'a non-Jewish region and the home of a non-Jewish Jesus'.[22] Of course, postcolonial critics regarded such readings of the Bible as smacking of imperial arrogance, and they conceived their task as being to de-Europeanize Jesus, placing him back in his own cultural context, divesting him of the Western appendages so enamoured by Eurocentric scholars.

Since Western scholars had traditionally controlled the interpretative agenda, their method of interpreting the biblical text was often deemed to be *the* normative approach by which all other methods were to be tested, and *the* benchmark against which all rival interpretations were to be judged. They tended to consider themselves as the true custodians of the interpretation of Scripture, and the implicit assumption was that interpretations emanating from Asia or Africa were somehow inferior.[23] Interpreters from the Third World were regarded as lacking the sophisticated exegetical tools deployed by Western scholars in the academy; theirs was an emotional, spontaneous response to the Bible, far removed from the detached, objective interpretation of their European counterparts.

While their analysis of the biblical text might be interesting and, at times, engaging, it lacked the required academic pedigree, and therefore was not to be taken too seriously. If they wanted their interpretations to gain credibility, they should endeavour to come to terms with the subtleties and complexities of the historical-critical method and conform to the rules, criteria and conventions established within the Western academic paradigm.

With the rise of postcolonial criticism, however, scholars from the Third World began to resist the notion that their Western counterparts had the sole authority to determine the text's meaning, and they steadfastly opposed European hegemonic control over biblical interpretation. Just as feminist biblical scholars had challenged patriarchal interpretations of the Bible, so black scholars began to question the assumptions and procedures of their European counterparts. They argued that the story of the Bible was *their* story, and that the events recorded on the pages of Scripture spoke directly and constructively to their own situation. They perceived echoes in the Bible of their own beliefs and rituals, for both worlds were inhabited by spirits, demons and angels, and both shared similar practices, such as polygamy and libation. Such echoes, far from being an impediment to biblical interpretation, were viewed as 'convenient prerequisites for entering the world of the Bible which was populated with similar notions and customs', and the affinities between the cultural and religious practices of ancient Israel and their own led them to claim that 'they had a special access to the texts denied to their counterparts in the West' (Sugirtharajah 2002: 58). Their own experience in the religious, social, political and economic realms could lead them to provide a distinctive and creative interpretation of the Bible, and may even enable them to discover and appreciate nuances in the biblical text which the learned exegete in the academy may have missed.[24] European scholars did not provide the only – or even necessarily the best – interpretation of Scripture. Indeed, the kind of scholarly readings of the Bible which emerged from Western academies was deemed by people in the Third World to be largely irrelevant to their needs, for it was completely alien to their lives and faith.

One feature of the pervasive Eurocentrism of biblical scholarship, which postcolonial critics highlighted, was the way in which they had neglected or denied the African 'presence' in the Bible.[25] This omission was addressed by some of the contributors to the volume *Stony the Road we Trod*, edited by Cain Hope Felder, a scholar who had been instrumental in advocating the programme of African–American biblical interpretation.[26] Eurocentric scholars, they argued, had consistently contrived to de-Africanize the Bible, or at least to regard the African presence in the text as secondary and unimportant. To make up for this omission, emphasis was placed on the African characters who featured in Scripture, such as the Queen of Sheba (1 Kgs 10.1–13), the Ethiopian eunuch (Acts 8.26–40) and Simon of Cyrene, who helped Jesus carry his cross (Mt. 27.32; Lk. 23.26). In Acts 13.1, Simeon, a black man, was part of the leadership of the church in Antioch, which suggests the racial pluralism of the nascent Christian church. Moreover, many passages in the Old Testament made favourable reference to black people: in the days of Hezekiah, Israel hoped that Tirhakah, the king of Ethiopia, would intervene and stave off the impending Assyrian assault by Sennacherib (Is. 37.9; 2 Kgs 19.9); Jer. 46.9 refers to the mighty men of Ethiopia and Put who carried the shield; the prompt action of an Ethiopian saved Jeremiah's life (Jer. 38.7–13) and, as a result, he became the beneficiary of a divine blessing (Jer. 39.15–8). Thus, instead of occluding the presence of Africans in the Bible, biblical scholars should recognize that the Israelites held African nations in high regard and admired them for their military strength and political stability. Indeed, one of the contributors to the volume went so far as to claim that 'if an Israelite wished to show approval of something or someone, favorable comparison to Africans was one way of doing that' (Bailey 1991: 183).

Much work remains to be done on the complicity of Western scholars with colonialism and the extent to which factors such as racism played a role in the development of modern biblical scholarship. The work of African-American scholars serves as a timely reminder of the prevalent Eurocentric bent of biblical scholarship and it is clear that their interpretation of the Bible has instilled in them a new sense of national pride and purpose. In doing so, they claim to have recaptured the ancient biblical vision of racial and ethnic pluralism, and by focussing on the black presence in the Bible they maintain that 'Africans were part of salvation history even before Western missionaries introduced Christianity to the continent' (Sugirtharajah 2002: 59).

Conclusion

Although comparatively few biblical scholars have engaged seriously with postcolonial theory, its practitioners have generally found it to be a useful tool to further scholarly inquiry. R. S. Sugirtharajah, by far the most able and prolific exponent of postcolonial studies in relation to the Bible, claims that its application to biblical studies has 'both energized and enraged the discipline' (2006a: 7). It has energized the discipline by opening up new avenues of scholarly investigation, inviting biblical studies to work in tandem with a range of other disciplines. Moreover, by placing the colonial 'other' at the centre of academic discourse, it has brought to the fore often neglected aspects of well-known texts and transformed our under-standing of long familiar passages. But postcolonial criticism has also enraged the discipline, for it has challenged the dominant interpretation of Western scholars and destabilized received read-ings of the text. Not surprisingly, it has been viewed by some as a threat to the traditional interpretation of Scripture, for its adher-ents have subverted the comfortable academic certainties of the past and questioned mainstream conclusions and the conventional patterns of biblical scholarship.

It will be obvious from the above discussion that postcolonial criticism shares a similar agenda and similar goals to feminist biblical criticism discussed in Chapter Two.[27] Both recognize the existence of a plurality of oppressions in the biblical text, based on class, gender and ethnicity; both seek to restore memories and events hitherto suppressed, neglected or overlooked; both reclaim voices that have been silenced or ignored; both share a commit-ment to the social and political empowerment of the marginalized and oppressed; both are acutely aware that the writing of history is a task performed by the winners and that protest voices are seldom registered in the extant tradition; and, finally, both exploit the sub-versive elements of Scripture and appreciate the liberating potential of the Bible. In doing so, they have often succeeded in undermining and transforming mainstream white, male, Western understanding of the Bible and correcting what they regard as the misinterpreta-tion and misrepresentation of the biblical text.[28]

Moreover, postcolonial criticism has focussed attention on an uncomfortable truth, namely, that the Bible is both a problem and a solution. It has highlighted the inevitable difficulties that arise when both oppressor and oppressed share the same sacred text, but in doing so it has underscored the multifarious nature of the Bible, for it is a book that endorses freedom and enslavement, deliverance and conquest. The same Bible was used as a tool by the colonizer to justify imperial rule and by the colonized to motivate resistance to oppressive domination. Such ambivalence and ambiguity clearly presents the interpreter with a challenge, for it serves as a reminder that the Bible sometimes emits conflicting messages and that passages can be quoted to justify opposing viewpoints.

R. S. Sugirtharajah has warned that those who have experienced the legacy of colonial rule at first hand should not arrogate to themselves the sole prerogative of engaging in postcolonial criticism. It is important that scholars in the West also place issues relating to colonialism and imperialism at the centre of intellectual inquiry, for it is a method that faces up to the challenge of re-reading ancient texts in a way that sometimes produces new and unexpected results. It also serves as a timely reminder that all readers bring to the biblical text their own experience and their own conceptual frames of reference, and that our own reading of the Bible is wonderfully enriched by people engaging with the text from different perspectives and different social locations. For that reason, postcolonial criticism will probably continue to exercise influence for years to come within the safe haven of biblical scholarship.

CONCLUSION

The field of biblical studies is constantly expanding to accommodate new methods of scholarly inquiry, and the four approaches discussed in this volume are but a small selection of the methodologies currently deployed by scholars as a means of enriching our understanding of the biblical text. In this concluding chapter, it is our aim to provide a brief overview of three other scholarly approaches that seem to the present author to have made a significant impact on the way in which the Bible is currently interpreted, namely, rhetorical criticism, canonical criticism and ethical criticism. These strategies are not unrelated to those discussed in the preceding chapters. For example, our discussion of ideological criticism suggested that the biblical writers were able to manipulate their readers to share their perspective and concur with their point of view; rhetorical criticism merely takes this a step further by investigating the methods which they adopted in order to present their case and advance their argument. Our discussion of feminist criticism and postcolonial criticism suggested how certain biblical texts were taken out of context in order to undermine the feminist cause or provide justification for colonial expansion; canonical criticism may be regarded as providing a welcome corrective to such skewed readings of the Bible by prioritizing the canon and showing how our perception of particular issues may be modified by viewing the Bible as a coherent, integrated whole. Finally, our chapter on reader-response criticism emphasized the need to respond to the text in a variety of ways, but it did not focus sufficiently on the ethical ramifications of particular texts within the Bible; hence the importance of applying to the biblical text what may be termed 'ethical criticism'.

Rhetorical criticism

The case for applying rhetorical criticism to the Bible was first advanced by James Muilenburg in his presidential address to the Society of Biblical Literature in 1968, entitled 'Form Criticism and Beyond'.[1] Muilenburg did not repudiate form criticism as a valid method of scholarly inquiry – indeed, he regarded himself as a form critic – but he was aware of its limitations and believed that the historical-critical approach had led to a neglect of the study of the books of the Bible as a coherent literary whole.[2] The problem with form criticism, as Muilenburg saw it, was that it tended to lay 'such stress upon the typical and representative that the individual, personal and unique features of a particular pericope are all but lost to view' (1969: 5). The challenge facing biblical scholars, therefore, was to move 'beyond form criticism' and to broaden their vision by examining the rhetorical arrangement of the text and how the component parts had been configured to achieve maximum rhetorical effect.[3] The effect of Muilenburg's address was to add another 'criticism' to the repertoire of the biblical scholar, namely, 'rhetorical criticism', and the last 40 years or so have witnessed a veritable explosion of publications examining the rhetorical impact of various biblical passages or biblical books.[4]

But while Muilenburg's address undoubtedly signalled a significant shift in biblical research, rhetorical study of the Bible was by no means new. Classical rhetoric as developed in ancient Greece and Rome influenced the early Church Fathers, and Augustine, for example, believed that the letters of Paul had been influenced by classical rhetorical style (see Tull 1999: 156–7). Interest in the subject of rhetoric continued throughout the Middle Ages, and the rhetoric of Paul's epistles was discussed by the Reformers in the fifteenth and sixteenth centuries CE. Although there was something of a lull in interest in rhetoric after the Reformation,[5] it became popular again in German biblical scholarship between the late eighteenth and early twentieth century. The resurgence of interest in rhetoric towards the end of the twentieth century, following Muilenburg's lead, resulted in numerous publications on both the Old and New Testaments. New Testament rhetorical critics were fortunate in having at their disposal various handbooks teaching rhetorical technique, which began to emerge from the fifth century BCE onwards, which conveniently provided examples of literary artistry contemporaneous with the time during which the New Testament documents were written.[6] The Old Testament scholar, however, is hampered by the lack of any textbooks on ancient Hebrew rhetoric which might have proved useful to establish what constituted literary artistry in ancient Israel. Although some clues may be gained from ancient Near Eastern sources, the Old Testament scholar must glean as much as possible about ancient Israelite literary style from the Old Testament texts themselves.

At a very basic level, rhetoric is about the art of persuasion.[7] In common parlance the term is sometimes used dismissively to suggest that a particular argument is vacuous, unconvincing or insubstantial (as, for example, in phrases such as 'this is mere rhetoric' or 'it is long on rhetoric and short on substance');[8] however, as used by biblical scholars, the term has been restored to full respectability and is used in a more neutral way to refer to the literary artistry of a biblical book or biblical passage and the way in which the authors have used various literary devices to achieve their goal. Thus rhetorical criticism is not simply a study of the writers' style but the techniques that they used to manipulate their readers, to argue their case, and to persuade their audience of the validity of their argument.

At this point it may be useful to consider two biblical texts, one from the New Testament and one from the Old, in order to illustrate how rhetorical critics might approach the passages in question.

The passage that we shall consider from the New Testament is 1 Corinthians 9.1–10.13, where Paul seeks to argue for the right of apostles (himself included) to be supported financially by members of the church. The first step for the rhetorical critic is to determine the extent of the rhetorical unit to be studied. It seems reasonable to regard 1 Cor. 9.1–10.13 as a self-contained unit, since it represents a digression from the argument about food offered to idols in chapter 8, which is resumed again in 10.14; in principle, however, the rhetorical unit could have been taken to include 1 Corinthians as a whole, or the entire Corinthian correspondence, or even the entire Pauline corpus.[9] The second step is to define the 'rhetorical situation', that is, the particular circumstance that prompted the writer to respond in this way. This is important, for we must

remember that in reading Paul's letters we are, in effect, eaves-
dropping on one side of a conversation only; to properly appreciate his argument we must attempt a hypothetical reconstruction
of his supposed dialogue partners. For example, did some of the
Jewish converts to Christianity in the Corinthian church object
to the apostle taking money for providing spiritual instruction
when no rabbi would have considered doing so? Or did some of
the members of the church view the apostle as little better than the
wandering sophists who regularly took a fee for delivering lectures
on issues of moral concern? Having decided what the situation
was that called forth Paul's utterance in this unit, the third step is
to analyse the style, the ordering of the various components, and
the way in which the argument is constructed. Paul begins with a
series of rhetorical questions: 'Am I not an apostle? Have I not seen
Jesus our Lord?' (v. 1), thus making clear at the very outset that
he is speaking with the authority of an apostle commissioned by
Christ himself; indeed, should his readers have any doubts about
his status, the very fact that the Corinthian church existed should
be proof enough of his apostolic authority ('Are you not my work in
the Lord? If I am not an apostle to others, at least I am to you; for
you are the seal of my apostleship in the Lord'; vv. 1–2). Paul then
appeals to established cultural norms that he expects his readers to
share in order to strengthen his argument: do not those who engage
in military service, or who tend the vineyards, or who look after
their flocks deserve payment for what they do (v. 7)? If this general
case can be conceded, then surely the particular right of apostles to
receive financial support for their labours is entirely justified. But
Paul's argument is also based on the authority of the Torah ('Does
not the law also say the same?'; v. 8), and by appealing to Moses'
law, he effectively debunks any potential oppositional claims that
his arguments depend merely on 'human authority'. Thus the case
that Paul puts before his readers seems clear-cut and is summed up
succinctly in v. 11: 'If we have sown spiritual good among you, is it
too much if we reap your material benefits?'

As an example from the Old Testament, we might consider
Amos' oracles against the nations in Amos 1.3–2.16. In this case, it
is easy enough to delimit the unit, for it consists of a series of threats
directed first at Israel's neighbours (Damascus, Gaza, Tyre, Edom,
Ammon and Moab) and concludes with oracles against Judah and
Israel. Form critics have long pointed out that all the oracles follow

a similar pattern: each is introduced by the same phrase ('Thus says the LORD'; vv. 3, 6, 9, 11, 13; 2.1, 6), followed by an accusation (using the formula 'for three transgressions . . . and for four'), and concludes with the threat of punishment. But while form critics were concerned with identifying which of these oracles were authentic utterances, which could be attributed to Amos himself,[10] rhetorical critics were far more interested in addressing issues of a different kind. Why does the prophet begin with a series of oracles against Israel's neighbours and then suddenly turn to denounce his own people? How would his oracles have been perceived by his contemporaries? Why does he use the expression – which seems odd to contemporary readers – 'for three transgressions . . . and for four'? Why does he appeal to well-known traditions from Israel's earlier history (2.9–10)?

Rhetorical critics point out that to begin with oracles denouncing Israel's neighbours for their war crimes was an effective means of ensuring a hearing from the people; the prophet was doing precisely what his audience would have expected him to do, namely, cursing the traditional enemies of Israel. Indeed, one can imagine the delight that would have accompanied the prophet's stern denunciation of the foreign nations, and the nod of approval at the sentence imposed upon them by Yahweh. No doubt, as the oracles proceeded the assent would have been ever more enthusiastic. The audience would have appreciated the rhetorical flourish represented by the expression 'for three transgressions . . . and for four', for the prophet was suggesting that one such sin committed by the nations would have been bad enough, but they had committed three or four of them! But while his audience would surely have expected the oracles against the nations to serve as a precursor to an oracle of salvation directed at Israel, the prophet – no doubt to the sheer surprise and dismay of his audience – concludes by turning to condemn his own people. Indeed, there follows a much more detailed description of the offences committed by Israel, which included corruption in the administration of the law, oppression of the poor, and participating in a degenerate cult (vv. 6–8). The implication is that the social and religious evils found within Israel are just as serious in Yahweh's eyes as the international crimes committed by the other nations. Instead of the usual threat of punishment that follows the list of crimes committed, the oracle directed against Israel contains a reminder of Yahweh's graciousness towards his people in the past ('Also I brought you up out of the land of Egypt, and led you forty years in the wilderness, to possess the land of the Amorite'; 2.10), which was clearly designed to make Israel's crimes appear even more culpable than those of the surrounding nations. Consequently, the punishment described in 2.13–18 is all the more severe: Israel had shown themselves to be no better than their neighbours whom they would have been quick enough to condemn. Further, the previous oracles against the surrounding nations had already prepared the prophet's audience to face an unpalatable truth, namely, that no-one who had sinned could hope to escape punishment, and this point is elaborated at great length in 2.14–16 with reference to the people of Israel:

> Flight shall perish from the swift,
> and the strong shall not retain their strength,
> nor shall the mighty save their lives;
> those who handle the bow shall not stand
> and those who are swift shall not save themselves,
> nor shall those who ride horses save their lives;
> and those who are stout of heart among the mighty
> shall flee away naked in that day, says the LORD.

Thus the pattern deployed in 1.3–2.5 is modified in 2.6–16 for rhetorical effect, and the entire unit 1.3–2.16 indicates a skilful progression of thought so that the condemnation of Israel at the end of the series achieves maximum effect.

Similar examples to those cited above could be provided for substantially larger units of text, including entire books within the Bible (see Trible 1994; van der Lugt 1995). Clearly, Muilenburg's inspiring presidential address has borne fruit, for it has guided scholars to appreciate biblical texts as works of art in their own right, and to recognize that the inner workings of a particular passage, including such stylistic features as repeated motifs and patterns, are there for a specific purpose, namely, to persuade the original audience or contemporary reader to accept the validity of the argument being presented. By applying rhetorical criticism to the Bible, we inevitably come from the text with a heightened appreciation of the subtlety with which the biblical writers or editors have established their case, and with an awareness that they knew much more about how to construct a logical and cogent argument than modern critics have often supposed.

Canonical criticism

One of the main exponents of the canonical critical approach to Scripture was Brevard Childs who, in numerous publications, argued that the Bible could only properly be appreciated theologically and ethically when account was taken of the full range of the biblical witness.[11] As we read the Bible, we must constantly bear in mind the meaning and import of the biblical message as a whole, and eschew any attempt to privilege any particular portion of it. For adherents of this strategy, no hermeneutic can be regarded as satisfactory that does not take into account all parts of Scripture and make allowance for the different emphases encountered in its manifold traditions. It was therefore incumbent upon the reader to 'hear the full range of notes within all of Scripture' (Childs 1970: 163), just as it was incumbent upon the exegete 'to sketch the *full range* of the Biblical witnesses within the canonical context that have bearing on the subject at issue' (132; his italics). Reading the Bible must involve the elucidation of the whole in relation to its parts and its parts in relation to the whole, and the significance of individual statements must be measured in the context of the entire thrust of biblical revelation. Canonical criticism demands that Scripture be viewed as a unified, organic entity, and it requires the reader to respect the overarching perspective and character of the tradition in its entirety. Thus the plea of those who adopt the canonical approach is quite straightforward: let us not try to elicit theological or ethical norms from isolated texts but look, rather, at the broader picture and go by the general impression of the biblical message as a whole. Scripture establishes certain norms and values as acceptable and others as unacceptable, and whatever impression is left by individual incidents or provisions, there is a 'general drift' to be discerned, which makes it abundantly clear what is required and what is prohibited.

In this regard, Childs believed that he was merely rehabilitating an exegetical tradition that had always existed in the church but one which had been largely ignored or abandoned with the rise of the historical-critical approach. That tradition had endeavoured to relate various parts of the Bible to one another and to work consistently from the context of the whole canon. Such a tradition could be traced back to the early Church Fathers, who had worked in conscious awareness of the canonical dimensions of the text, and who had struggled to find ways of dealing theologically with the Old and New Testaments as part of the canon of Scripture. In the period of the Reformation, Luther had similarly tried to come to terms with the relation between the two Testaments, and Calvin's exposition of the Psalms was admired by Childs because he brought 'the whole spectrum of Biblical teaching to bear on a particular verse' (1970: 145). Childs was at pains to emphasize that the canonical approach which he advocated was not a return to a pre-critical period of Bible study; nevertheless, he believed that the writings of the early Church Fathers and the great classics of the Reformed and Lutheran post-Reformation tradition provided a welcome antidote to the one-sided emphasis of much contemporary biblical scholarship, preoccupied as it was with the development of the biblical literature and the separating of the 'original' material from the 'secondary'.

In order to appreciate how the canonical approach might work in practice, we may briefly examine Childs' discussion of the book of Amos (1979: 395–410). Childs observes that most of the book consists largely of denunciations by the prophet against Israel and the nations (1.3–2.16), and against the rich and powerful who exploit and oppress the weak and impoverished (5.10–13; 6.4–7). At the end of the book, however, there is a 'sudden shift from a message of total judgment for Israel to one of promise' (1979: 405), and instead of announcing the complete destruction of the northern kingdom (see 7.7–9; 8.1–3; 9.1–4), attention now focuses on a message of hope and future prosperity that will accompany the restoration of the Davidic dynasty (9.11–15). Commentators usually assume that the oracle contained in Am. 9.11–15 does not represent the 'genuine' words of the prophet Amos but is, rather, a later addition to the book supplied by subsequent editors. Yet, the book of Amos as we have it today is a single text, and Childs insists that it must be read as such if we are properly to grasp the import of its message. No matter that the closing verses do not represent the words of the historical Amos; the point is that the final oracle of salvation modifies the message of the rest of the book and alters the significance of the previous oracles of judgement. God now emerges as redeemer

as well as judge, and the divine punishment is proclaimed to be neither inevitable nor irrevocable. Viewed in terms of the book's final
canonical shape, the message of judgement is transformed into one
of hope and promise for all future generations, and the 'original'
words of Amos are seen in a broader framework, which transcends
the perspective of the prophet himself. The later embellishments,
therefore, are not to be dismissed as distorting accretions which
can conveniently be put to one side; rather, they are an essential aid
to understanding the proper construal of the book's message. In
effect, the final composition of the book serves as a check and control over any assessment of its meaning, and provides a reminder
that its basic message is found not in any individual passage but in
the complimentarity established by the book as a whole. The goal
of the interpreter, therefore, should not be to recover the 'original'
message of Amos himself, or the original setting of his oracles, but
to discern how, in the final composition of the book, 'the message
of Amos was appropriated and formed to serve as authoritative
scripture within the community of faith' (Childs 1979: 400).

Further, the application of canonical criticism may serve to neu-
tralize the force of offending passages in the Bible. Thus, for example, texts that appear to incite hatred and intolerance towards the
enemy are mitigated by those that command love of one's neigh-
bour (Lev. 19.18); passages that reflect an unfavourable attitude
towards foreign nations (Deut. 23.3–6, 20) are tempered by those
that exhibit a concern for the needs of the stranger and resident
alien (Exod. 22.21; 23.9). In a similar fashion, passages that depict
the wrath of God (see Exod. 32.9–11; Num. 11.10, 33) must be
seen in the light of his ample manifestations of love and grace (see
2 Chr. 7.3, 6); texts that portray him as a vengeful and bloodthirsty
deity (see Deut. 7.1–2) must be set alongside those that depict him as
patient, long-suffering and slow to anger (see Exod. 34.6); passages
that cast him as fickle and capricious (see 2 Sam. 24.16; Jer. 18.8)
must be understood in the context of those that depict the basic
consistency of his purpose and the unchangeableness of his character (see 1 Sam. 15.29; Mal. 3.6). By viewing different texts alongside one another, emphasis is placed on the totality of Scripture
and on the interaction between various parts of the canon, and
this serves to mitigate some of its more objectionable passages, for,
in the last resort, it is not isolated passages that make the ethics of

the Bible distinctive and normative, but the way in which different biblical passages are seen to cohere and interrelate.

It is easy to understand the appeal of canonical criticism for biblical scholars, for it is a strategy that is in tune with recent trends in biblical research, where the traditional 'atomistic' approach to Scripture is increasingly giving way to studies that focus on large sections of the biblical text, including entire books, whatever the original date and authorship of their individual components. Moreover, it represents an approach to the Bible which gives the impression of fullness, completeness and balance. The hermeneutic principle that undergirds it seems perfectly sound and logical: only by recognizing the whole range of biblical testimony, and discovering the general drift of Scripture, are we likely to arrive at sensible, balanced conclusions regarding the teaching of the Bible. To focus too narrowly on selected texts only leads to a distortion of the moral and theological witness of the Bible, and encourages readers to seek a warrant for a particular viewpoint, or justification for a particular action, by referring to a specific verse or passage within Scripture. It thus guards against the danger of evaluating the subject-matter of the Bible in a way that is pre-determined to be ultimately positive or negative, and provides the ultimate antidote to selective appeals to favourite proof-texts. Readers cannot twist the biblical message to mean what they want it to mean, or blow some bits out of proportion to fit some preconceived position of their own. Since the meaning or significance of a particular passage might change when viewed in its wider canonical context, Scripture must be read as an integrated and coherent whole, and the emphasis must be on the total impression gained when the variety of viewpoints expressed in the Bible are taken into account.

But although canonical criticism has undoubtedly opened up new interpretative possibilities, and has much to contribute to current debates about ways of interpreting the Bible in general, the strategy is not without its potential drawbacks. While adherents of this approach are able to tell us *what* we ought to do (viz., read each passage of the Bible in the context of the whole), and *why* we should do it (viz., so that we can view a particular biblical text in its wider perspective), they do not tell us *how* we should do it. How are ordinary readers expected to take cognizance of the totality of Scripture? Indeed, will they be sufficiently *au fait* with the content of the Bible as a whole to be able to do justice to the complexity and diversity of its moral witness? Thus one of the main problems with canonical criticism is its practical implementation, for the task of recovering the totality of the biblical message in order to do justice to its parts is not one that the ordinary reader of Scripture can easily undertake. While one may well agree that, in principle, the Bible must be allowed to speak for itself in the full range and variety of its teachings, the process of discerning what scholars refer to as the 'main thrust' or 'general drift' of Scripture is not as simple as canonical critics would like to suppose. The fact is that when people read the Bible they do not normally contemplate the existence of multiple witnesses within the canon, and still less do they pause to ponder on the nature of their relation to one another. Reading the Bible with an eye to its wholeness is a perfectly laudable aim, but it is a task that is easier said than done.

Furthermore, the canonical approach implies that we can discern an 'ethos' or 'general drift' in the theological and moral worldview of the Bible, and that when we consider a particular issue within the context of the entire canon, a kind of consensus can be seen to emerge. The danger of this approach, however, is that it produces a harmonistic levelling out of the diversity and distinctiveness of the various parts of the Bible, so that the text of Scripture is made to speak with a single voice. For example, some scholars have argued that the basic 'thrust' of the biblical teaching is a message of peace, love and forgiveness, and they refer to passages depicting the harmony associated with the coming Messianic kingdom, and the teaching of Jesus concerning love of enemies. The effect of such an argument, however, is to give the impression that violence is only an incidental or peripheral feature of the Bible, whereas, in fact, it is a dominant theme in many books contained in the Old Testament. The canonical approach raises the expectation that the various traditions of the Bible will cohere and that the different voices will come together to form a reasonably harmonious choir, but in doing so it often attempts to systematize the unsystematizable, and the plurality of perspectives is dissolved in an attempt to achieve a harmony where patently no harmony exists.

Despite these reservations, however, canonical criticism may have much to contribute to ways of reading and understanding the Bible. Recent studies on the book of Isaiah, for example, have demonstrated how a fresh appreciation of the material can emerge when isolated passages are viewed in the context of the book as a whole. Canonical criticism serves as a salutary reminder that texts can prove mutually illuminating, and that inter-textual dialogue can often help the reader to penetrate the deeper significance of a particular passage and appreciate its fuller implications.

Ethical criticism

Ethical criticism may be regarded as a branch of reader-response criticism, but its emphasis is on the ethical ramifications of the biblical text. Ethical critics maintain that readers of the Bible have a right – and, indeed, a duty – to probe, question and oppose statements that seem to them to be morally unacceptable. Far from being passive recipients of the text, they are encouraged to become active agents whose duty it is to subject the ethical implications of the Bible to critical scrutiny. Adherents of this approach argue that the attitude of scholars towards the biblical text in the past has tended to be empathetic and consensual, rather than suspicious and critical, and readers have been more prone to defend and affirm the values enshrined in the Bible rather than to question and critique them. Instead of examining the underlying assumptions of the biblical writers, scholars have tended to assume a deferentially uncritical attitude to the text of Scripture, and have simply aligned themselves with the dominant voice of the text.

A striking example of the failure of commentators to question the morality of the ethically problematic texts of Scripture may be seen in a fairly random sample of commentaries on Genesis 19.[12] This chapter recounts how two angels in human form visited Sodom and were invited by Lot to stay in his house overnight (vv. 1–3). While they were there, however, the men of Sodom surrounded the house and threatened to rape the guests (vv. 4–5). Lot sought to protect them by offering his own daughters to the angry mob and suggesting that they rape them instead (vv. 6–8). Faced with this chilling account, commentators almost marvel at Lot's willingness to allow his own daughters to be violated rather than permit the homosexual rape of two strangers who happened to be staying under his roof. For example, John Skinner commended him as 'a courageous champion of the obligations of hospitality', and claimed that the action that he took was 'to his credit'

(1930: 307). Bruce Vawter suggested that Lot was 'more sensitive to the duties of hospitality than those of fatherhood', and in case we should be unduly perturbed by Lot's behaviour, he reassuringly informs us that such action 'would not have seemed as shocking to the ancient sense of proprieties as it may seem to our own' (1977: 235–6). Indeed, he concluded that there was 'no need to make excuses' for Lot, since he was basically 'a good not a bad man' (236). Von Rad in his commentary on Genesis was similarly anxious to come to Lot's rescue by suggesting that his action in offering his own daughters to be raped 'must not be judged simply by our Western ideas' (1972: 218), and A. S. Herbert rather lamely attempted to exonerate Lot's behaviour by reminding his readers that Lot had, after all, been living in Sodom, where 'a weakening of his moral judgement' may have taken place (1962: 46). Such examples could easily be multiplied, but the striking element is the reticence of commentators to pass judgement on Lot's actions. Instead of condemning him for offering his daughters as rape victims, they sympathize with his predicament and point to mitigating circumstances (such as the oriental respect for hospitality) in order to excuse his behaviour. What biblical scholars have signally failed to do is to apply to the text of Scripture the kind of ethical critique that scholars such as Wayne Booth (1988), Terry Eagleton (1978) and J. Hillis Miller (1987) have applied to secular literature. The failure of biblical commentators to pass moral judgment on such passages as Genesis 19, and their tendency to remain passive, unperturbed, and non-committal in the face of such gratuitous violence, is nothing less than an abdication of their responsibility as biblical exegetes. There is certainly no shortage of passages in the Bible – in the New Testament as well as the Old – that call for moral critique, and if biblical scholarship is not to remain insular and self-serving, it must articulate clearly the ethical ramifications of such texts, and the concrete implications of the kind of ideology that they promote.

The above brief overview of scholarly approaches to Genesis 19 suggests that biblical commentators have traditionally had little appetite for engaging in a detailed critique of the values inherent in the biblical text. They have been quite prepared to question the historical accuracy or reliability of the biblical traditions, but have shied away from questioning the validity of its moral norms and ethical assumptions. They have usually proceeded from an examination of the text to an explanation of its meaning without pausing for a moment to pass judgement on its content. As a result, the task of evaluation has all but been evacuated from the realm of biblical criticism. David J. A. Clines has taken his fellow academics to task for their unwillingness to emerge from the safe haven of descriptive discourse in order to engage openly in the tasks of evaluation and critique:

> Not one academic biblical scholar in a hundred will tell you that their primary task is to *critique* the Bible. For some reason, we have convinced ourselves that our business is simply to *understand*, to *interpret*. Here we have some difficult texts from the ancient world, we say, rightly enough. Do you want to know what they *mean*? Then come to us, we are the experts, we *understand* them, we shall tell you how to *interpret* them. But don't ask us for *evaluation*, for *critique*. Oh no, we are objective scholars, and we prefer to keep hidden our personal preferences and our ethical and religious views about the subject matter of our study (1997: 23; his italics).

While it is probably true to say that ethical criticism has yet to make its full impact upon the realm of biblical study, it is no less true that an important aspect of the discipline is denied if we refrain from exercising moral critique. As James Barr has remarked: 'How much would the study of an ancient thinker like Plato have been impoverished if throughout the ages scholars had confined themselves to expounding the text and its internal semantic linkages and had rigorously excluded from their minds the question: "Is Plato right?"' (Barr 1980: 25). It is a sad indictment of the discipline that ethical criticism has usually been dispatched to the margins of biblical study, for by suppressing their critical instincts scholars give the impression of being untroubled and unconcerned by the negative implications of the text that was the object of their study.

Some have no doubt been reluctant to engage in ethical criticism of the Bible because they accord the text of Scripture a privileged status which, in their view, should render it immune to criticism and correction; others have been wary of applying such an approach to the biblical text because they believe that it violates academic norms of objectivity. It must be remembered, however, that moral critique is something that is encountered within the biblical tradition itself. In Abraham's debate with God concerning the proposed destruction of Sodom, or in Job's restless questioning of the divine justice, profound questions are raised within the Bible concerning the very nature and character of God. The biblical writers recognized that if the traditions of ancient Israel were to remain meaningful, they had to be rigorously appraised, and had to maintain their value and relevance in the face of critical questioning. It is therefore arguable that the application of 'ethical criticism' to the biblical text does not involve the introduction of an alien principle into biblical interpretation; on the contrary, the warrant for this strategy is that it is precisely the kind of process that is evident within the biblical tradition itself.

*   *   *

In this volume, we have attempted to explain the distinctive characteristics of some of the contemporary approaches to the Bible and to outline the various factors that have contributed to the development of each method. We have also indicated some of the intellectual currents that have generated and guided each approach, and suggested ways in which they have served to illuminate the social, class, gender and racial issues at work in the text. It is clear that biblical criticism has been heavily influenced by trends in cultural and literary theory, and there is now a general recognition among scholars that study of the Bible cannot function in isolation from other disciplines. But nor can it function in isolation from the social and intellectual world of the interpreter, for our understanding of the Bible is inevitably determined by our experience, our ethnic identity, our sexual orientation, our economic status and institutional context. It is for this reason that much contemporary biblical criticism is concerned not only with understanding a particular text but also with understanding our own working assumptions as we interpret the text.

The profile of biblical studies is constantly changing and the various approaches discussed in the preceding chapters provide ample testimony that the Bible retains the power to offer new challenges, to raise new questions and to elicit new answers. Indeed, it is doubtful if the discipline has ever been more healthy, creative and diversified as it is at present. But, of course, a study of contemporary approaches to the Bible must never become a substitute for reading the Bible itself. For this reason, the words of Richard G. Moulton,[13] written over a century ago, are as relevant today as they were then:

> We have done almost everything that is possible with these Hebrew and Greek writings. We have overlaid them, clause by clause, with exhaustive commentaries; we have translated them, revised the translations, and quarrelled over revisions; we have discussed authenticity and inspiration, and suggested textual history with the aid of colored type; we have mechanically divided the whole into chapters and verses, and sought texts to memorise and quote; we have epitomised into handbooks and extracted school lessons; we have recast from the feminist point of view, and even from the standpoint of the next century. There is yet one thing left to do with the Bible: simply to read it.

NOTES

INTRODUCTION

1 Some scholars have questioned the appropriateness of the designation 'historical-critical method', since not all studies that went under this appellation were specifically 'historical', and studies that *were* historical were not always particularly critical; see Nissinen 2009: 480–1. Moreover, it is arguable that there is no such thing as the historical-critical *method*, only methods (in the plural) used by historical critics, such as source-, textual-, form- and redaction-criticism. The singular form is used here for convenience rather than in the interests of terminological accuracy. For a balanced assessment of the historical-critical method, see Barton 2007: 31–68.

2 In the 1970s, W. Wink complained that no one could make a career in biblical scholarship unless they stuck steadfastly to the historical-critical paradigm (1973). By the 1990s, the opposite was the case and, as James Barr has commented, 'anyone who professes his or her main interest to lie in the source analysis of the Pentateuch is somewhat unlikely to obtain an academic post' (2000: 17).

3 Books and articles appeared bearing such titles as *The End of the Historical Critical Method* (G. Maier 1974); 'Will the Historical-Critical Method Survive? Some Observations' (Keck 1980: 115–27); 'Historical Criticism: Are its Days Numbered?' (Clines 2009). Barton has claimed that when the *Cambridge Companion to the Bible* was being planned, some suggested that there was no need for the inclusion of a chapter on the historical-critical approach, since this was now so obviously entirely *passé* (1998: 2).

4 Barr argues that tradition and continuity in biblical scholarship should be prized and preserved as far as possible; indeed, he feels that 'too much of the recent discussion has involved a fevered grasping at innovation and a willingness to make a quick abandonment of what earlier scholarship had achieved' (2000: 180).

5 The appearance of J. P. Fokkelman's *Narrative Art in the Genesis* (1975) is generally regarded as an important landmark, since it was the first detailed study to apply the new-critical insights to the biblical narratives.

6 See Gerald West, who argued that because academics engaged in the study of the Bible were primarily accountable to the guild of biblical scholars, 'many of the questions asked of the biblical text are not those being asked by ordinary people' (1995: 50).

7 The term 'savage text' is used by Adrian Thatcher to refer not to the Bible as a whole but to 'what Christians have made of the Bible when they have used its pages to endorse cruelty, hatred, murder, oppression and condemnation, often of other Christians', so that Christianity comes to represent a faith that 'customizes hatred' (2008: 5).

CHAPTER ONE

1 For two exemplary anthologies of the writings of reader-response critics, both of which contain excellent annotated bibliographies, see S. R. Suleiman and I. Crosman (1980) and J. P. Tompkins (1980).

2 See Hirsch 1967: 1–23 and 1976: 17–92 for his robust defence of the privileged status of authorial meaning.

3 For Hirsch's distinction between 'meaning' and 'significance', see Hirsch 1976: 1–13.

4 Some critics, aware that the author's intention was ultimately an ideal construct, which could never be retrievable, preferred to speak instead of the 'inferred intention' of the author. See S. Mailloux 1982: 94–108.

5 Even Hirsch was prepared to concede that 'authors are sometimes very inept explainers of their meanings' (1967: 6). Significantly, Hirsch failed to produce a single example of an ambiguous literary text the meaning of which was cleared up by the author's extra-textual explanation. See R. Crosman 1980: 156.

6 As R. Wellek and A. Warren observe, many instances of glaring misinterpretations by an author of his own work exist, and the anecdote about Browning professing not to understand his own poem probably contains an element of truth (1984: 148).

7 Indeed, examples could be cited of authors discerning a range of different meanings in a work that they themselves had composed. R. Crosman (1980: 151–4) refers to Ezra Pound's explication of the meaning of his two-line poem 'In a Station of the Metro' in his volume *Gaudier-Brzeska* (1916: 100–3), in which the poet himself discerns several meanings in his own poem.

8 Fish's theory concerning the 'interpretive community' was first introduced in his essay 'Interpreting the *Variorum*', in which he tried to account for the variety as well as the stability of readers' responses to a text (1980: 147–80).

9 Even some recent biblical critics are reticent to dispose of the notion of authorial intent and argue that it can be a legitimate goal of exegetical study, although such an argument is frequently accompanied by two provisos: first, that a more nuanced account of 'intentionality' is required than was previously found in scholarly literature; second, the author's intention should not be regarded as the only hermeneutic principle when it comes to interpreting a literary text. See M. G. Brett 1991: 1–16; L. Alonso Schökel 1998: 28–39.

10 The historical-critical method may appear ostensibly to be text-oriented, but as Barton observes, 'the original author in some sense is the place where the method comes to rest' (1996: 240–1).

11 For a brief survey of the developments in biblical studies which precipitated a shift of emphasis from author to text to reader, see D. J. A. Clines 1990: 9–12.

12 For examples of 'reader-response' approaches to the Bible, see R. Detweiler 1985; E. V. McKnight 1989; J. Cheryl Exum and D. J. A. Clines 1993; R. S. Briggs 2010; M. A. Powell 2011; M. Lieb et al. 2011. Mention should also be made of the new journal published by Sheffield Phoenix Press, *Biblical Reception*, edited by Cheryl Exum and D. J. A. Clines.

13 For a discussion of the way in which feminist biblical critics have appropriated the insights of reader-response criticism, see my volume, *The Dissenting Reader: Feminist Approaches to the Hebrew Bible* (2003).

14 As R. Morgan and J. Barton (1988: 292) observe, the reason both Christians and Jews find as much agreement as they do in the interpretation of the Bible is that the tradition and life of their respective communities provide some guidance concerning the meanings that may be deemed acceptable and appropriate.

15 For much of what follows, see the detailed discussion by Fowler (1996).

16 Fowler regards the various repetitions encountered in the course of the gospel as 'discrete episodes in a thoughtfully constructed narrative' (1996: 141). He objects to the term 'doublets', commonly used to describe duplications of a similar narrative, preferring instead the expression 'matched pair'.

17 A similar point is made by Tannehill, who notes that 'the Gospel is open-ended, for the outcome of the story depends on decisions that the church, including the reader, must still make' (1977: 404; quoted by Fowler 1996: 259).

18 Fowler 1996: 250. Fowler maintains that 'how the reader responds to the end of Mark's Gospel is what the end of Mark's Gospel is about' (248).

CHAPTER TWO

1 The quotations are taken from Sarah Moore Grimké's *Letters on the Equality of the Sexes and Other Essays*, in the version edited by E. A. Bartlett (1988: 38). The volume originally appeared in 1838 under the title *Letters on the Equality of the Sexes, and the Condition of Woman*, Boston: Isaac Knapp.

2 For a discussion of Cady Stanton's contribution to feminist biblical studies, see Wacker (1998: 3–7) and Schüssler Fiorenza (1993: 1–24).

3 The contributors to *The Postmodern Bible* argue that the work situates Cady Stanton as an 'extraordinarily troubling emblem for white feminism', on account of its explicitly racist rhetoric (1995: 236). Opposition to *The Woman's Bible* came even from the National American Suffrage Association (ironically co-founded by Cady Stanton) which, in its 28th annual convention convened in 1896, officially repudiated any connection with the project, no doubt anxious not to offend its more conservative membership.

4 The situation scarcely improved during the opening decades of the twentieth century: in 1930 just 8 per cent of the SBL membership was made up of women; by 1940 it had fallen to 6 per cent, and a decade later it had fallen further still to 5 per cent. See Bass 1982: 9.

5 A representative sample of some of the more significant contributions may be found in the ten volumes edited by A. Brenner under the title, *A Feminist Companion to the Bible*; see, also, *A Feminist Companion to Reading the Bible: Approaches, Methods and Strategies* (ed. by A. Brenner and C. Fontaine).

6 Schüssler Fiorenza 1999: 3, 33. In an earlier volume, she recounts the following telling recollection: 'As one of my colleagues remarked about a professor who had written a moderate article on women in the Old Testament: "It is a shame, she may have ruined her scholarly career"' (1983: xvi). Non-feminists have been quick to point out that Schüssler Fiorenza's complaint that women are discriminated against

academically on account of their interest in feminist biblical criticism seems a bit rich coming from one who held a prestigious Chair at Harvard University!

7 Daly's first book, *The Church and the Second Sex* (1968) was written when she was a member of the Catholic church, but, as time went on, she lost all patience with the slow pace of ecclesiastical reform, and in *Beyond God the Father* she began to outline the case against all forms of Christianity, especially Roman Catholicism.

8 Renita J. Weems, for example, while admitting her ambivalent attitude towards the Christian tradition, concedes that 'as a scholar committed to scholarship that serves liberation purposes my very vision of what a just, equitable, humane and righteous world order looks like is deeply influenced by the utopian imagination and impulses from my Judeo-Christian upbringing' (2006: 30).

9 For example, Ann Loades admits that her contribution on 'Feminist Interpretation' in *The Cambridge Companion to Biblical Interpretation* (ed. by J. Barton) 'assumes a willingness to continue to struggle, but in full consciousness of the very real difficulties to be encountered' (1998: 82).

10 Elsewhere, Schüssler Fiorenza uses the term 'creative revision' to describe her method of retelling, or re-writing, the biblical stories from a feminist perspective; such a method enables her to '*create* narrative amplifications of the feminist remnants that have survived in the biblical texts' (1985b: 135; my italics).

11 Even Loades, while applauding Schüssler Fiorenza's outstanding contribution to feminist interpretation of the New Testament, concedes that 'it may be, indeed, that her hope for the future leads her to find more in the early Christian movement than can justifiably be claimed' (1998: 90).

12 Bal sets out her position regarding the Bible as follows: 'I do not claim the Bible to be either a feminist resource or a sexist manifesto. That kind of assumption can be an issue only for those who attribute moral, religious or political authority to these texts, which is precisely the opposite of what I am interested in. It is the cultural function of one of the most influential mythical and literary documents of our culture that I discuss, as a strong representative instance of what language and literature can do to a culture, specifically to its articulation of gender' (1987: 1).

13 Indeed, Ruether argues that feminist scholars such as Mary Daly, who have rejected the Bible outright, have missed 'the essential dynamism and conflict of biblical religion and the dialectic of its own internal self-critique and development' (1982: 59).

14 The very prophets who articulated such powerful visions of social justice also contributed some of the most blatantly misogynistic texts in the Old Testament. Some prophetic texts imply that women are by nature deviant and promiscuous and that female desire is motivated by lust rather than by love (see Jer. 2.20–5). Moreover, the prophetic use of sexual imagery is regarded by some feminist biblical scholars as bordering on the obscene (e.g. Hos. 2.3, 10; Jer. 13.20–7; Ezek. 16.35–52; 23.11–21; see Setel 1985: 86–95; Dijk-Hemmes 1993: 162–70).

15 The article was originally published in German under the title, 'Ist voraussetzungslose Exegese möglich?' in *Theologische Zeitschrift* 13 1957: 409–17; it subsequently appeared in English translation in R. Bultmann, *New Testament and Mythology and other Basic Writings*, 1985: 145–53.

16 'Womanist' was a term coined by Alice Walker (1983: xi): 'Womanist: From womanish (opp. of "girlish" . . .) A black feminist or feminist of color. From the black folk expression of mothers to female children, "You acting womanish", like a woman. Usually referring to outrageous, audacious, courageous or wilful behaviour'. Although 'womanist criticism' is a relatively recent phenomenon, some have argued that it is deeply rooted in the intellectual and political climate of the nineteenth century and that its origins predate those of white feminist criticism (see Caraway 1991: 117–67). For an understanding of the historical context that gave rise to the emergence of black feminist consciousness, see Cannon 1985: 30–40.

17 Osiek (1985: 94) admits that the work of womanist scholars serves as 'an indictment of the middle-class feminists of recent years for their failure to see beyond their own horizons'.

18 Barton refers to Trible's oft-cited article, 'Bringing Miriam out of the Shadows', and observes that few feminist critics have taken the trouble to bring Moses' Cushite wife 'out of the shadows' (2006: 166).

CHAPTER THREE

1 P. D. Miller's contribution to the *Festschrift* presented to G. E. Wright (1976) represents a significant and early recognition of the role of ideology in the Old Testament.

2 Norman Gottwald's monumental work *The Tribes of Yahweh* (1979) remains one of the most impressive ideological analyses of biblical religion. His approach is heavily influenced by Marxist ideology.

Equally impressive is Meir Sternberg's *The Poetics of Biblical Narrative* (1985), which represents a triumph of close reading of the biblical text. Other important contributions include those of James Barr (2000), Mark Zvi Brettler (1995), W. P. Brown (1993), David J. A. Clines (1995), S. Japhet (1989), D. Jobling and T. Pippin (1992), Tina Pippin (1996), Iain W. Provan (1995) and K. W. Whitelam (1989).

3 Barr 2000: 140. Barr argues that those who use the term 'seem to have only a very poor, vague, and confused idea of what they are trying to say' (140). In his view, ideology is an 'obnoxious term' (101) and when used negatively its effect is usually to 'create a great rubbish heap upon which texts are tossed, one after the other, without their being given proper value or examination' (129).

4 Eagleton (1991: 1–2) and Clines (1995: 10–11) list various definitions of the term. These include 'ideas which help legitimate a dominant political power'; a 'body of ideas characteristic of a particular social group or class'; a 'socially necessary illusion'; 'ideas that are often unexpressed and unrecognized by those who hold them'; 'ideas that are wrongly passed off as natural, obvious or commonsensical'. Examples of most of these will be found in the course of the present chapter.

5 It is in this sense that the word is often used in contemporary political discourse in order to discredit opposing views.

6 Whitelam (1989: 121) suggests that such threats might have come from two quarters, namely, groups that had been forced to cede their arable lands to the king, and the urban élite who might want to usurp royal power and privilege.

7 Whitelam (1989: 130–1) notes that this emphasis on the dual role of the king as judge and warrior was common throughout the ancient Near East and was found particularly in the royal literature of Egypt and Mesopotamia.

8 Jobling (1992: 95–127) argues that Ps. 72 represents a subtle but intentional ideology to benefit the élite class that used the psalm in the liturgy.

9 See Lemche (1978: 2–25). Brettler has persuasively argued that there can be no doubt that a royal Davidic ideology existed in ancient Israel; indeed, he goes so far as to claim that 'we can be more certain of the existence of that ideology than of the existence of David as a ruler of a Judean state!' (1995: 143). Whitelam (1984) includes the entire narrative complex 1 Sam. 9–2 Kgs 2 under the title 'the defence of David' in recognition of the fact that the material in these chapters is clearly royal propaganda. His view stands in sharp contrast to the earlier argument of von Rad, who regarded 2 Sam. 9–20; 1 Kgs 1–2

as objective reports such as might have been provided by an 'impartial onlooker' to the events (1965: 166–204). Of course, that von Rad should have come to such a conclusion is testimony to the skill of the narrator who managed to keep his real agenda concealed from the reader.

10 Brettler (2005: 107–8) believes that the story was originally told about Elhanan and was secondarily transferred to David on the basis of the principle usually followed by historians, namely, that if two sources each attribute the same action (especially a heroic one) to a well-known figure and to one who was otherwise unknown, it probably originally related to the latter and was later transferred to the former in order to make his status even more elevated. See Herrmann 1975: 138–39.

11 Brettler 1995: 107. David was not, of course, unrelated to Saul, since he was his son-in-law through his marriage to Michal, Saul's daughter (1 Sam. 18.17–27). But lest his entry into the royal family lay David open to the charge of opportunism, the narrator is careful to suggest that the initiative with regard to David's marriage was taken by Saul. Indeed, this afforded the narrator with a further opportunity to denigrate Saul's character, since he was able to imply that Saul's permission for David to marry his daughter was merely a clever ruse on Saul's part, for he set the bride-price at a hundred Philistine foreskins in the expectation that David would surely be killed while collecting them (vv. 17, 25).

12 Such royal propaganda was by no means limited to ancient Israel. Brettler (1995: 94–7) shows how Assyrian annals deployed literary devices to serve ideological aims, the scribe carefully selecting and reworking his source material in order to glorify the Assyrian king, Sargon. He notes that much of the depiction of history in Mesopotamia was propagandistic and apologetic and was largely controlled by the court scribes who wrote an account of events that would satisfy the ruling king. In a similar vein, Whitelam (1984: 71) notes that the same type of propaganda is found in the 'apology of Hattusili III', designed to justify the seizure of the Hittite throne by an usurper. Interestingly, he points to examples where the Hittite scribes legitimize the new king by denigrating previous regimes, traditions that show a striking parallel to the account in 1 Sam. 9–1 Kgs 2 of David's rise to power.

13 Whitelam (1984: 61–78) argues that the books of Samuel are permeated throughout with a pro-Davidic ideology, but, as Brettler observes, a strong pro-Davidic ideology would surely have omitted the David/Bathsheba debacle altogether, as does the Chronicler, who narrates the capture of Ammon (1 Chron. 20.1–3) but studiously omits any reference to David's adultery. Brettler notes that this should 'remind

us of the power of ancient historians to ignore or rewrite events which disagreed with the ideology they wished to convey' (1995: 97–8).

14 Whitelam (1984: 63–5) emphasizes that in the establishment of political power the successful use of all available media was important, since manipulation by force of arms alone was seldom sufficient for the ruler of a regime to maintain control over the population. While most scholars have focussed on the use of literature to influence the outlook of the audience, Whitelam emphasizes the importance of non-literary factors in the propagation of royal propaganda. He suggests, for example, that such features as the pyramids of Egypt and the temple/palace complex and royal fortifications in Jerusalem following Solomon's reign would have served as a visible sign of the ruler's legitimacy and authority. Given that literacy in this period would in all probability have been restricted to an élite minority, it is arguable that the graphic and non-linguistic material would have been even more significant than the literary, since the propaganda value of this would have 'penetrated to most levels of Israelite society' (64).

15 See Lemche, who claims that the presence of ideological motives in these narratives suggests that they must be 'of dubious value as a historical source for the earlier history of David' (1978: 3). Similarly, Whitelam observes that the seemingly 'realistic' picture of the intrigues and struggles involving David is due 'not to the objective standpoint of the author(s), but rather the defensive nature of court apologetic' (1984: 70).

16 This work comprises Deuteronomy and the four books known as the Former Prophets, namely, Joshua, Judges, Samuel and Kings. That these books are the product of the same authors/editors is evident from the similarity between them as regards vocabulary, style, theology and ideology.

17 Carroll argues that the failure to treat Omri adequately is a good indication of the ideological nature of the biblical text and 'a serious mark against its historical reliability' (1997: 95–6).

18 David Clines (1995) has led something of a crusade to expose not only the ideology of the text but also the hidden agendas and tacit presuppositions of the scholars who interpret the biblical text.

19 Davies 1992: 31. Thompson similarly draws a distinction between 'critical academic scholarship' and 'religiously and theologically motivated biblical interpretation' (1992: 13).

20 Whitelam (1986: 45–7) also finds the similarities of approaches in recent reconstructions of the 'history of Israel' (such as those by Noth,

Bright, de Vaux and Herrmann) quite 'disturbing', since they contain no explicit reference to the assumptions that underlie their approaches to the study of history. Whitelam argues that there is now a surfeit of writings on Israel's history covering much the same ground.

21 S. Reif (1998: 143–59) similarly argues that the religious commitment of scholars has inevitably influenced the way they have interpreted the biblical text. He notes that most scholars engaged in teaching and researching the Old Testament in institutions of Higher Education in Europe and North America are practising Christians and that, despite the rise of modern biblical criticism, their religious convictions continue to impact on their theological presuppositions, particularly their tacit assumption that the Old Testament is fulfilled the New.

22 A similar point is made by Lemche, who makes the following observation: 'We may therefore ask whether scholars have not too easily accepted the role of spokesmen for the basically anti-Canaanite attitude of the biblical writers, thereby preventing themselves from forming their own unprejudiced opinions of Canaanite life and culture' (1991: 16).

CHAPTER FOUR

1 It is generally recognized that the work that paved the way for postcolonial criticism was Edward Said's influential volume, *Orientalism*, which was published in 1978. Said took the term 'orientalism' to refer to the Western way of 'dominating, restructuring, and having authority over the Orient' (Said 1978: 3, quoted by Sugirtharajah 2002: 15). Two other influential figures in the development of postcolonial theory were Homi Bhabha and Gayatri Spivak, though the Bible plays only a marginal role in their writings.

2 Nobody has written more extensively or more eloquently on postcolonial theory as it relates to biblical studies than R. S. Sugitharajah, who was, by all accounts, the first to introduce postcolonial criticism to biblical studies in an article published in the *Asia Journal of Theology* in 1996 (see Sugirtharajah 2006: 72). The present chapter owes much to his outstanding contribution to this aspect of biblical research. See, especially, the volumes published in 1998 (ed.); 1999 (ed.); 2001; 2002; 2006a (ed.); 2006b (ed.). For an admirable survey of the field and an introduction to some of its leading practitioners, see Sugirtharajah 2002: 11–42; 2006: 64–84.

3 Weems (1993: 33–4) notes that it is only within the last hundred years or so that African Americans in large numbers have been able

to read for themselves; prior to that time, the content of the Bible was mediated to their enslaved ancestors orally, and naturally the slave masters selected only those passages of Scripture that would have served their own interests.

4   Michael Prior has provided a very useful discussion of 'the use of the Bible as a legitimization for the implementation of an ideological, political programme, the consequences of which have been, and continue to be, the irreversible suffering of entire communities and, in some cases, their virtual annihilation as a people' (1997: 14).

5   Alexander the Great is said to have drawn his inspiration for empire-building from the literary characters depicted in *The Iliad*; indeed, he is reported to have carried a copy of it on his conquest journeys and 'kept it under his pillow together with a dagger' (Quint 1993: 4, quoted by Dube 2006: 298).

6   West (1995: 52) comments that in the South African context the Bible was used 'as both an instrument of social control and an instrument of social struggle'.

7   Dube regards the narrative as the product of the Johannine community, and views it as part of the missionary vision of that community (2006: 304).

8   The confusion with regard to the name is generally regarded as due to a later editorial revision of the text, which attempted to combine separate sources.

9   Other rabbis traced the black colour to Cain and regarded it as his punishment for offering an unsuitable sacrifice; see Midrash Rabbah on Gen. 22:6. See Copher 1991: 148–9.

10 Prior notes that this narrative, although important for the programme of colonization generally, was regarded as particularly significant for the existence of the Jewish state: 'Many Jews allege an unique derivative link between the biblical paradigm of 'conquest and Zionist settler colonialism today. If other forms of colonization could appeal to the alleged legitimization provided by the biblical mandate, the Jewish claim was unrivalled' (1997: 185).

11 It should be noted that historians of ancient Israel have long disputed the extent to which the biblical conquest narratives correspond to events that actually happened, and a variety of hypothetical reconstructions have been suggested to account for the so-called 'conquest of Canaan' (see Ramsey 1981: 65–98). The narrative of the conquest remains highly problematic, however, even if it is not historically reliable, for people are shaped and moulded by reading the text as it is, not as learned scholars would like it to be read. Besides, the narrative itself is

far more potent and powerful than any hypothetical reconstruction, which would be familiar to very few anyway. See, further, Davies 2010: 18–20.

12 Some have detected in recent decades a resurgence of the idea of America as the 'new Israel' and as the divinely appointed guardian of justice and freedom in the world (Horsley 2008: 2–3). Gottwald (2008: 23) regards such an equation as 'grotesque in the extreme', since it deceptively overlooks the enormous political and military power of the US compared to the politically weak condition of ancient Israel. Gottwald suggests that if any analogies are to be drawn, the US would more nearly correspond to the great empires of Egypt, Assyria, Babylon, Persia and Rome, while ancient Israel would be comparable to relatively weak and powerless countries such as Cuba, Chile, Nicaragua and Iraq (23–4).

13 See Prior 1997: 282. The sermon of Cotton Mather, delivered in Boston in 1689 charged the members of the armed forces in New England to regard themselves as Israelites marching through the wilderness and being ready to confront the Amalekites. It was their duty to cast out the Indians 'as dirt in the streets' and eliminate them from memory. See Prior 1997: 263.

14 See Ariarajah 2006: 355. For a discussion of this command in the light of a 'parallel' text from the Buddhist tradition, see Soares-Prabhu 2006: 331–46.

15 Martin (1991: 206–31) notes the far-reaching effect these texts had on the lives of African Americans, for in the eighteenth and nineteenth centuries they were frequently quoted by white pro-slavery apologists and their sympathizers, who claimed that the submission of black slaves to their white masters was something mandated by Scripture. For example, Charles Hodge's essay, published in 1860, appealed directly to the Household Codes to justify the submission of slaves to their master: 'The obedience which slaves owe their masters, children their parents, wives their husbands, people their rulers, is always made to rest on the divine will as its ultimate foundation. It is part of the service which we owe to God' (quoted in Martin 1991: 213).

16 R. A. Warrior, a member of the Osage nation of American Indians, provides a Native American liberation reading of the conquest narrative in which the Native Americans are identified with the Canaanites, 'the people who already lived in the promised land' (2006: 237). N. S. Ateek (1989), writing as a Palestinian Christian, similarly highlights the hermeneutical problem that an excessive emphasis on the exodus entails, for the freedom of the Hebrews from Egypt was secured precisely so that they could conquer another's territory.

17 D. Tollerton has argued that, while liberation theologians such as Gustavo Gutiérrez were politically radical, they were, in fact, theologically quite conservative (2007: 70–91).

18 Prior 1997: 283. Anthony Thiselton has also criticized liberation theologians for manipulating the biblical text to provide only positive signals for the aspirations and desires of those whom they represent: 'Any merely selective use of texts to encourage those who are oppressed can be perceived in principle to represent precisely the same strategy of hermeneutical method as the oppressors who use texts to legitimize their own programmes . . . Without some critical hermeneutical tool, both sides in the struggle can continue to appeal to different texts to re-enforce and re-affirm their corporate identity and interests' (1992: 429).

19 See, especially, the valuable essays in the volume edited by Horsley 2008.

20 Although there is no definite information in the Old Testament regarding the rate of interest charged in ancient Israel, it is known that in Babylon during the first dynasty it was about 20–25 per cent on money and about 33.3 per cent on grain (Driver and Miles 1952: 176). Leemans (1950: 32–3) notes that this rate of interest was not unduly high, since in a land as agriculturally productive as Babylonia, the farmer would have had a good return on his crop. In Assyria, it appears that the lender had a free hand in determining the rate that he wished the borrower to pay, but as a rule it may be said that the interest on money ranged between 20 and 80 per cent per annum, and the interest on grain might be as high as 50 per cent per annum. See Mendelsohn 1932: 10–11; Davies 1981: 66–9.

21 Brett observes a tension in the prophets between their condemnation of the hubris of empires such as Assyria, Babylon and Persia on the one hand, and, on the other, the prophetic visions of the future, which use imperial imagery to describe Israel taking over other nations. Brett asks: 'How is Israel's possession of the nations different from the Ammonite sin of 'enlarging her border' (Amos 1.13) or the arrogance of imperialist Assyria when it says 'I have removed the borders of the peoples' (Isa. 10.13)?' (2008: 102).

22 Moxnes 2001: 26. Their argument was based on the presupposition that Galilee, where Jesus grew up, was far removed from the centre of Judaism, and that this region was not, in fact, Jewish, since its ethnic composition was made up of Phoenicians, Syrians, Arabs and even Greeks. The aim was clearly to distance Jesus from the Judaism of his day. Since the nineteenth century was so influential in establishing the

nature of subsequent biblical scholarship, it is not surprising that such an understanding of Jesus' ethnic background should have persisted into the twentieth century. In Nazi Germany, the issue of the race and identity of the Galileans became a special focus of interest, since the supposed 'Jewishness' of Jesus posed an acute problem. The problem was overcome by suggesting that Galilee, owing to its cultural diversity and the ethnic composition of its inhabitants, was a part of Palestine that was not identified with Judaism. As Moxnes notes, 'it became, if not quite a "little Germany", at least a place where there were enough Aryans to make Jesus a plausible non-Jew' (2001: 33). Moreover, Susannah Heschel (2008) has demonstrated how German Protestant theologians, during the Third Reich, were motivated by racism and, tapping into traditional Christian anti-Semitism, redefined Jesus as an Aryan, and Christianity as a religion that was at war with Judaism. For a detailed discussion of the way in which the racial values of modern imperial Europe and the US have influenced the discipline of modern biblical scholarship, see Kelley 2002.

23 For examples of such exegetical hubris, see Sugirtharajah 2002: 75–9.

24 Carlos Mesters (1989) has shown how ordinary people in the base communities in Brazil frequently saw nuances in the biblical text which had escaped academics in the West.

25 Kelley has noted that Hegelian biblical scholarship and those influenced by Hegelian biblical scholarship effectively erased Africans from the biblical world; hence, 'it is one of the crucial tasks of African–American biblical scholars to recover what has been rendered invisible and to see the Africans who do appear in the text' (2002: 66).

26 The title of the volume was taken from the Negro national anthem, 'Lift Every Voice and Sing', and it was regarded as epitomizing the struggle of African–American scholars who engage in biblical interpretation.

27 Kwok Pui-lan (2005) has focussed attention on both postcolonial theory and feminist biblical criticism and has shown how the former can open up new avenues for studying gender relations in early Christianity. See, also, the volume edited by Laura E. Donaldson and Kwok Pui-Lan (2002).

28 This is not to deny that tensions sometimes emerge between the two disciplines. For example, feminist biblical critics sometimes complain that postcolonial criticism is too male-centred and overlooks the role of women in emancipatory struggles, while some feminists in the Third World accuse their counterparts in the West of failing to problematize the colonial agenda embedded in the biblical text.

CONCLUSION

1 The address was published in the following year in the *Journal of Biblical Literature* (1969). As John Barton has observed, there are not many movements in biblical studies whose beginnings can be exactly dated, but this is one of them (1996: 199). One of the contributors to the *Festschrift*, which was to be presented to Muilenburg on the occasion of his 78th birthday, regarded his presidential address as 'the crowning climax of his career' and correctly predicted that he had pressed 'the frontier of biblical studies into new regions which will be explored further in years to come' (Anderson 1974: ix). Regrettably, Muilenburg died on 10 May 1974, a few days before the presentation of the *Festschrift* was due to be made.

2 As Tull observes, the very fact that Muilenburg was himself a highly regarded form critic enabled him to articulate its shortcomings in convincing ways, and his position as President of the Society of Biblical Literature conferred an element of legitimation to the new direction in biblical studies which he was advocating (1999: 160).

3 Muilenburg's commentary on Second Isaiah in the *Interpreter's Bible* (1956) evinced a particular sensitivity to the rhetorical features of the prophecy and its structured argumentation.

4 Among works published on stylistic features of the biblical text, mention may be made of the volumes by J. P. Fokkelman (1975; 1981); D. M. Gunn (1978; 1980); S. Bar-Efrat (1989); R. Alter (1981); and M. Sternberg (1985); see, also, the volumes edited by J. J. Jackson and M. Kessler (1974); D. J. A. Clines et al. (1982); R. Alter and F. Kermode (1987); D. Patrick and A. Scult (1990). For discussions of rhetorical criticism in relation to the New Testament, see D. E. Aune (2004); C. J. Classen (2000); B. L. Mack (1990); S. E. Porter and D. L. Stamps (2002); and W. Wuellner (1987). For a comprehensive bibliography of works on rhetorical criticism of the Bible up until 1994, see Watson and Hauser (1994).

5 Tull suggests that the decline in interest in rhetoric during this period was due to the rise of scientific inquiry, as increasing emphasis came to be placed on observable, verifiable fact rather than logic and persuasion (1999: 157).

6 Some scholars have argued that Paul's letters, in particular, exhibit a wealth of rhetorical techniques, and they have raised the possibility that he may have received formal training in rhetoric (see Betz 1979).

7 Aristotle defined 'rhetoric' as 'the art of discovering the best possible means of persuasion in regard to any subject whatever' (quoted by Winterowd 1968: 14).

8 John Locke famously defined rhetoric as 'that powerful instrument of error and deceit'.

9 For a discussion of 1 Corinthians 9.1–10.13 from a rhetorical–critical perspective, see *The Postmodern Bible*, 1995: 149–86.

10 Most commentators agree that the oracle against Judah in 2.4–5 is a later addition on account of the fact that the prophet is not otherwise concerned with Judah in his utterances; doubts have also been raised concerning some of the other oracles. The general consensus is well expressed by Barton, when he concludes that 'the Judah oracle is certainly, the Edom oracle almost certainly, and the Tyre oracle very probably, not by Amos; the other oracles are authentic words of the prophet' (1980: 24).

11 Childs' arguments were first outlined in detail in 1970 in a volume entitled *Biblical Theology in Crisis* in which he argued that previous scholarly approaches had been too atomistic and analytical, and had not been sufficiently concerned with the unity and totality of Scripture. A biblically based theology, according to Childs, must involve a 'disciplined theological reflection of the Bible in the context of the canon' (122). Childs did not deny the validity of the historical-critical approach, but believed that its adherents had dissipated their energies on speculative reconstructions that served only to detract attention from the texts themselves; in the process, they had ignored the function of the final shape of the canonical texts within the community of faith.

12 For what follows, see Davies 2003: 104–5.

13 Moulton 1900: iii–iv (quoted by Sugirtharajah 2001: 276).

BIBLIOGRAPHY

Alter, R. (1981), *The Art of Biblical Narrative*, London: George Allen & Unwin.

Alter, R. and Kermode, F. (eds) (1987), *The Literary Guide to the Bible*, London: Collins.

Anderson, B. W. (1974), 'The New Frontier of Rhetorical Criticism', in J. J. Jackson and M. Kessler (eds), *Rhetorical Criticism: Essays in Honor of James Muilenburg*, Pittsburgh, Pennsylvania: The Pickwick Press: ix–xviii.

Ariarajah, S. W. (2006), 'Interpreting John 14:6 in a Religiously Plural Society', in R. S. Sugirtharajah (ed.), *Voices from the Margin: Interpreting the Bible in the Third World*, Maryknoll, NY: Orbis Books: 355–70.

Ateek, N. S. (1989), *Justice, and Only Justice: A Palestinian Theology of Liberation*, Maryknoll, NY: Orbis Books.

Aune, D. E. (2004), *The New Testament and Early Christian Literature and Rhetoric*, Louisville, KY: Westminster John Knox Press.

Bailey, R. C. (1991), 'Beyond Identification: The Use of Africans in Old Testament Poetry and Narratives', in C. H. Felder (ed.), *Stony the Road we Trod: African American Biblical Interpretation*, Minneapolis: Fortress Press: 165–84.

Bal, M. (1987), *Lethal Love: Feminist Literary Readings of Biblical Love Stories*, Bloomington: Indiana University Press.

— (1988), *Death and Dissymmetry: The Politics of Coherence in the Book of Judges*, Chicago: Chicago University Press.

— (1990), 'Dealing/With/Women: Daughters in the Book of Judges', in R. M. Schwartz (ed.), *The Book and the Text: The Bible and Literary Theory*, Oxford: Basil Blackwell: 16–39.

Bar-Efrat, S. (1989), *Narrative Art in the Bible* (*JSOTSup* 70), Sheffield: Almond Press.

Barr, J. (1980), *The Scope and Authority of the Bible*, London: SCM Press.

— (2000), *History and Ideology in the Old Testament: Biblical Studies at the End of a Millennium*, Oxford: Oxford University Press.

Barton, J. (1980), *Amos's Oracles against the Nations*, Cambridge: Cambridge University Press.

— (1996; 2nd edn), *Reading the Old Testament: Method in Biblical Study*, London: Darton, Longman & Todd.

— (2007), *The Nature of Biblical Criticism*, London and Louisville, KY: Westminster John Knox Press.

Barton, J. (ed.) (1998), *The Cambridge Companion to Biblical Interpretation*, Cambridge: Cambridge University Press.

Barton, M. (2006), 'The Skin of Miriam became as White as Snow: The Bible, Western Feminism and Colour Politics', in R. S. Sugirtharajah (ed.), *Voices from the Margin: Interpreting the Bible in the Third World*, Maryknoll, NY: Orbis Books: 158–68.

Bass, D. C. (1982), 'Women's Studies and Biblical Studies: An Historical Perspective', *JSOT* 22: 6–12.

Bellis, A. O. (2000), 'Feminist Biblical Scholarship', in C. Meyers (ed.), *Discovering Eve: Ancient Israelite Women in Context*, Oxford and New York: Oxford University Press: 24–32.

Betz, H. D. (1979), *Galatians: A Commentary on Paul's Letter to the Churches in Galatia*, Philadelphia: Fortress Press.

Booth, W. (1988), *The Company we Keep: An Ethics of Fiction*, Berkeley: University of California Press.

Brenner, A. (1994), 'An Afterword: The Decalogue – Am I an Addressee?' in A. Brenner (ed.), *A Feminist Companion to Exodus to Deuteronomy*, Sheffield: Sheffield Academic Press: 255–8.

Brenner, A. and Fontaine, C. (1997), *A Feminist Companion to Reading the Bible: Approaches, Methods and Strategies*, Sheffield: Sheffield Academic Press.

Brett, M. G. (1991), 'Motives and Intentions in Genesis I', *JTS*, New Series, 42: 1–16.

— (2008), *Decolonizing God: The Bible in the Tides of Empire*, Sheffield: Phoenix Press.

Brettler, M. Z. (1995), *The Creation of History in Ancient Israel*, London and New York: Routledge.

— (2005), *How to Read the Bible*, Philadelphia: Jewish Publications Society.

Briggs, R. S. (2010), *The Virtuous Reader: Old Testament Narrative and Interpretive Virtue*, Grand Rapids, MI: Baker Academic.

Bright, J. (2000; 4th edn), *A History of Israel*, London: SCM Press.

Brown, W. P. (1993), *Structure, Role and Ideology in the Hebrew and Greek Texts of Genesis 1:1–2:3*, SBL Dissertation Series 132, Atlanta, GA: Scholars Press.

Bultmann, R. (1985), *New Testament and Mythology and other Basic Writings* (ed. and trans. by Schubert M. Ogden), London: SCM Press.

Cannon, K. G. (1985), 'The Emergence of Black Feminist Consciousness', in L. M. Russell (ed.), *Feminist Interpretation of the Bible*, Philadelphia: Westminster Press: 30–40.

Caraway, N. (1991), *Segregated Sisterhood: Racism and the Politics of American Feminism*, Knoxville: University of Tennessee Press.

Carroll, R. P. (1990), 'Ideology', in R. J. Coggins and J. L. Houlden (eds), *A Dictionary of Biblical Interpretation*, London: SCM Press: 309–11.

— (1997), 'Madonna of Silences: Clio and the Bible', in L. L. Grabbe (ed.), *Can a 'History of Israel' be Written? (JSOTSup* 245), Sheffield: Sheffield Academic Press: 84–103.

Childs, B. S. (1970), *Biblical Theology in Crisis*, Philadelphia: Westminster Press.

— (1979), *Introduction to the Old Testament as Scripture*, London: SCM Press.

Classen, C. J. (2000), *Rhetorical Criticism of the New Testament*, Tübingen: Mohr Siebeck.

Clements, R. E. (ed.) (1989), *The World of Ancient Israel: Sociological, Anthropological and Political Perspectives*, Cambridge: Cambridge University Press.

Clines, D. J. A. (1990), *What Does Eve do to Help? And Other Readerly Questions to the Old Testament (JSOTSup* 94), Sheffield: JSOT Press.

— (1995), *Interested Parties: The Ideology of Writers and Readers of the Hebrew Bible (JSOTSup* 205), Sheffield: Sheffield Academic Press.

— (1997), *The Bible and the Modern World (The Biblical Seminar* 51), Sheffield: Sheffield Academic Press.

— (2009), 'Historical Criticism: Are its Days Numbered?' *Teologinen Aikakauskirja* 114: 29–33.

Clines, D. J. A., Gunn, D. M. and Hauser, A. J. (eds) (1982), *Art and Meaning: Rhetoric in Biblical Literature*, Sheffield: JSOT Press.

Coggins, R. J. and Houlden, J. L. (eds) (1990), *A Dictionary of Biblical Interpretation*, London: SCM Press.

Collins, A. Y. (ed.) (1985), *Feminist Perspectives on Biblical Scholarship*, Atlanta, GA: Scholars Press.

Copher, C. B. (1991), 'The Black Presence in the Old Testament', in C. H. Felder (ed.), *Stony the Road we Trod: African American Biblical Interpretation*, Minneapolis: Fortress Press: 146–64.

Crosman, R. (1980), 'Do Readers make Meaning?' in S. R. Suleiman and I. Crosman (eds), *The Reader in the Text. Essays on Audience and Interpretation*, Princeton: Princeton University Press: 149–64.

Cross, F. M., Lemke, W. E. and Miller, P. D. (eds) (1976), *Magnalia Dei: The Mighty Acts of God. Essays on the Bible and Archaeology in Memory of G. Ernest Wright*, New York: Doubleday.

Daly, M. (1968), *The Church and the Second Sex*, Boston: Beacon Press.
— (1973), *Beyond God the Father: Toward a Philosophy of Women's Liberation*, Boston: Beacon Press.
Davies, E. W. (1981), *Prophecy and Ethics: Isaiah and the Ethical Traditions of Israel* (*JSOTSup* 16), Sheffield: JSOT Press.
— (2003), *The Dissenting Reader: Feminist Approaches to the Hebrew Bible*, Aldershot: Ashgate Publishing Limited.
— (2010), *The Immoral Bible: Approaches to Biblical Ethics*, London and New York: T & T Clark International.
Davies, P. R. (1992), *In Search of 'Ancient Israel'* (*JSOTSup* 148), Sheffield: JSOT Press.
Detweiler R. (ed.) (1985), *Reader Response Approaches to Biblical and Secular Texts* (*Semeia* 31), Decatur, GA: Scholars Press.
Dijk-Hemmes, F. van (1993), 'The Metaphorization of Woman in Prophetic Speech: An Analysis of Ezekiel XXIII', *VT* 43: 162–70.
Donaldson, L. E. (ed.) (1996), *Postcolonialism and Scriptural Reading* (*Semeia* 75), Atlanta, GA: Scholars Press.
Donaldson, L. E. (1999), 'The Sign of Orpah: Reading Ruth through Native Eyes', in R. S. Sugirtharajah (ed.), *Vernacular Hermeneutics*, Sheffield: Sheffield Academic Press: 20–36.
Donaldson, L. E. with Kwok Pui-Lan (ed.) (2002), *Postcolonialism, Feminism, and Religious Discourse*, New York: Routledge.
Driver, G. R. and Miles, J. C. (1952), *The Babylonian Laws*, vol. 1, Oxford: Clarendon Press.
Dube, M. W. (2006), 'Reading for Decolonization (John 4.1–42)', in R. S. Sugirtharajah (ed.), *Voices from the Margin: Interpreting the Bible in the Third World*, Maryknoll, NY: Orbis Books: 297–318.
Eagleton, T. (1978), *Criticism and Ideology: A Study in Marxist Literary Theory*, London: Verso.
— (1991), *Ideology: An Introduction*, London and New York: Verso.
Exum, J. Cheryl (1985), '"Mother in Israel": A Familiar Figure Reconsidered', in L. M. Russell (ed.), *Feminist Interpretation of the Bible*, Philadelphia: Westminster Press: 73–85.
Exum, J. Cheryl and Clines, D. J. A. (eds) (1993), *The New Literary Criticism and the Hebrew Bible* (*JSOTSup* 143), Sheffield: Sheffield Academic Press.
Felder, C. H. (ed.) (1991a), *Stony the Road we Trod: African American Biblical Interpretation*, Minneapolis: Fortress Press.
— (1991b), 'Race, Racism and the Biblical Narratives', in C. H. Felder (ed.), *Stony the Road we Trod: African American Biblical Interpretation*, Minneapolis: Fortress Press: 127–45.
Fetterley, J. (1978), *The Resisting Reader: A Feminist Approach to American Fiction*, Bloomington and London: Indiana University Press.

Fish, S. E. (1972), *Self-Consuming Artifacts: The Experience of Seventeenth-Century Literature*, Berkeley, Los Angeles and London: University of California Press.

— (1980), *Is There a Text in this Class? The Authority of Interpretive Communities*, London and Cambridge, MA: Harvard University Press.

— (1989), *Doing What Comes Naturally: Change, Rhetoric, and the Practice of Theory in Literary and Legal Studies*, Oxford: Clarendon Press.

Fokkelman, J. P. (1975), *Narrative Art in Genesis: Specimens of Stylistic and Structural Analysis*, Assen: Van Gorcum.

— (1981), *Narrative Art and Poetry in the Books of Samuel: A Full Interpretation based on Stylistic and Structural Analyses. Volume I: King David II Samuel 9–20 & I Kings 1–2*, Assen: Van Gorcum.

Fowler, R. M. (1996), *Let the Reader Understand: Reader-Response Criticism and the Gospel of Mark*, Harrisburg, PA: Trinity Press International.

Garbini, G. (1988), *History and Ideology in Ancient Israel* (trans. by John Bowden), London: SCM Press.

Gottwald, N. K. (1979), *The Tribes of Yahweh: A Sociology of the Religion of Liberated Israel 1250–1050 BCE*, London: SCM Press.

— (2008), 'Early Israel as an Anti-Imperial Community', in R. A. Horsley (ed.), *In the Shadow of Empire: Reclaiming the Bible as a History of Faithful Resistance*, Louisville, KY: Westminster John Knox Press: 9–24.

Gottwald, N. K. and Horsley, R. A. (eds) (1993; rev. edn), *The Bible and Liberation: Political and Social Hermeneutics*, Maryknoll, NY: Orbis Books.

Grabbe, L. L. (1997), *Can a 'History of Israel' be Written? (JSOTSup* 245), Sheffield: Sheffield Academic Press.

Grimké, S. (1838), *Letters on the Equality of the Sexes, and the Condition of Woman*, Boston: Isaac Knapp.

Gunn, D. M. (1978), *The Story of King David: Genre and Interpretation (JSOTSup* 6), Sheffield: JSOT Press.

— (1980), *The Fate of King Saul: An Interpretation of a Biblical Story*, Sheffield: JSOT Press.

Gutiérrez, G. (1974), *A Theology of Liberation*, London: SCM Press.

Herbert, A. S. (1962), *Genesis 12–50*, London: SCM Press.

Herrmann, S. (1975), *A History of Israel in Old Testament Times* (trans. by John Bowden), London: SCM Press.

Heschel, S. (2008), *The Aryan Jesus: Christian Theologians and the Bible in Nazi Germany*, Princeton and Oxford: Princeton University Press.

Hirsch, E. D. (1967), *Validity in Interpretation*, New Haven and London: Yale University Press.

— (1976), *The Aims of Interpretation*, Chicago and London: University of Chicago Press.

Holland, N. N. (1975), *5 Readers Reading*, New Haven and London: Yale University Press.

Horsley, R. A. (ed.) (2008), *In the Shadow of Empire: Reclaiming the Bible as a History of Faithful Resistance*, Louisville, KY: Westminster John Knox Press.

Iser, W. (1972), 'The Reading Process: A Phenomenological Approach', *NLH* 3: 279–99.

— (1974), *The Implied Reader: Patterns of Communication in Prose Fiction from Bunyan to Beckett*, Baltimore: The Johns Hopkins University Press.

— (1978), *The Act of Reading: A Theory of Aesthetic Response*, Baltimore and London: The Johns Hopkins University Press.

— (1980), 'Interaction between Text and Reader', in S. R. Suleiman and I. Crosman (eds), *The Reader in the Text. Essays on Audience and Interpretation*, Princeton: Princeton University Press: 106–19.

Jackson, J. J. and Kessler, M. (1974), *Rhetorical Criticism: Essays in Honor of James Muilenburg*, Pittsburgh, Pennsylvania: The Pickwick Press.

Jameson, F. (1981), *The Political Unconscious: Narrative as a Socially Symbolic Act*, London: Methuen; New York: Cornell University Press.

Japhet, S. (1989), *The Ideology of the Book of Chronicles and its Place in Biblical Thought*, Frankfurt: Peter Lang.

Jauss, H. R. (1982), *Toward an Aesthetic of Reception* (trans. by T. Bahti), Minneapolis: University of Minnesota Press.

Jobling, D. (1992), 'Deconstruction and the Political Analysis of Biblical Texts: A Jamesonian Reading of Psalm 72', in D. Jobling and T. Pippin (eds), *Ideological Criticism of Biblical Texts (Semeia 59)*, Atlanta, GA: Scholars Press: 95–127.

Jobling, D. and Pippin, T. (eds) (1992), *Ideological Criticism of Biblical Texts (Semeia 59)*, Atlanta, GA: Scholars Press.

Kahl, B. (2008), 'Acts of the Apostles: Pro(to)-Imperial Script and Hidden Transcript', in R. A. Horsley (ed.), *In the Shadow of Empire: Reclaiming the Bible as a History of Faithful Resistance*, Louisville, KY: Westminster John Knox Press: 137–56.

Keck, L. E. (1980), 'Will the Historical-Critical Method Survive? Some Observations', in R. A. Spencer (ed.), *Orientation by Disorientation: Studies in Literary Criticism and Biblical Literary Criticism Presented in Honor of William A. Beardslee*, Pittsburgh: Pickwick: 115–27.

Kelley, S. (2002), *Racializing Jesus: Race, Ideology and the Formation of Modern Biblical Scholarship*, London and New York: Routledge.

Kirk-Duggan, C. A. (2006), 'Let my People Go!: Threads of Exodus in African American Narratives', in R. S. Sugirtharajah, *Voices from the Margin: Interpreting the Bible in the Third World*, Maryknoll, NY: Orbis Books: 258–78.

Lacocque, A. (1990), *The Feminine Unconventional*, Minneapolis: Fortress Press.

Leemans, W. F. (1950), 'The Rate of interest in Old-Babylonian Times', *RIDA* 5: 7–34.

Lemche, N. P. (1978), 'David's Rise', *JSOT* 10: 2–25.

— (1991), *The Canaanites and their Land: The Tradition of the Canaanites* (*JSOTSup* 110), Sheffield: JSOT Press.

LeMon, J. L. and Richards, K. H. (eds) (2009), *Method Matters: Essays on the Interpretation of the Hebrew Bible in Honor of David L. Petersen*, Atlanta, GA: Society of Biblical Literature.

Lieb, M., Mason, E. and Roberts, J. (2011), *The Oxford Handbook of the Reception History of the Bible*, Oxford: Oxford University Press.

Loades, A. (1998), 'Feminist Interpretation', in J. Barton (ed.), *The Cambridge Companion to Biblical Interpretation*, Cambridge: Cambridge University Press: 81–94.

Lugt, P. van der (1995), *Rhetorical Criticism and the Poetry of the Book of Job*, Leiden: Brill.

Mack, B. L. (1990), *Rhetoric and the New Testament*, Minneapolis: Fortress Press.

Maier, G. (1974), *The End of the Historical Critical Method*, St. Louis: Concordia Publishing House.

Mailloux, S. (1982), *Interpretive Conventions: The Reader in the Study of American Fiction*, Ithaca and London: Cornell University Press.

Marshall, I. Howard (1978), *The Gospel of Luke: A Commentary on the Greek Text*, Exeter: The Paternoster Press.

Martin, C. J. (1991), 'The *Haustafeln* (Household Codes) in African American Biblical Interpretation: "Free Slaves" and "Subordinate Women"', in C. H. Felder (ed.), *Stony the Road we Trod: African American Biblical Interpretation*, Minneapolis: Fortress Press: 206–31.

McKenzie, S. L. and Haynes, S. R. (eds) (1999; rev. edn), *To Each its Own Meaning: An Introduction to Biblical Criticism and their Application*, Louisville, KY: Westminster John Knox Press.

McKnight, E. V. (ed.) (1989), *Reader Perspectives on the New Testament* (*Semeia* 48), Atlanta, GA: Scholars Press.

Mendelsohn, I. (1932), *Legal Aspects of Slavery in Babylonia, Assyria and Palestine: A Comparative Study*, Williamsport: Bayard Press.

Mesters, C. (1989), *Defenseless Flower: A New Reading of the Bible*, Maryknoll, NY: Orbis Books.

Meyers, C. (1988), *Discovering Eve: Ancient Israelite Women in Context*, Oxford and New York: Oxford University Press.

— (2000), *Women in Scripture: A Dictionary of Named and Unnamed Women in the Hebrew Bible, the Apocryphal/Deuterocanonical Books, and the New Testament*, Grand Rapids, MI and Cambridge, UK: W.B. Eerdmans Publishing Company.

Míguez-Bonino, J. (2006), 'Marxist Critical Tools: Are they Helpful in Breaking the Stranglehold of Idealist Hermeneutics?' in R. S. Sugirtharajah (ed.), *Voices from the Margin: Interpreting the Bible in the Third World*, Maryknoll, NY: Orbis Books: 40–8.

Miller, J. Hillis (1987), *The Ethics of Reading: Kant, de Man, Eliot, Trollope, James, and Benjamin*, New York: Columbia University Press.

Miller, P. D. (1976), 'Faith and Ideology in the Old Testament', in F. M. Cross, W. E. Lemke and P. D. Miller (eds), *Magnalia Dei: The Mighty Acts of God. Essays on the Bible and Archaeology in Memory of G. Ernest Wright*, New York: Doubleday: 464–79.

Milne, P. J. (1997), 'Toward Feminist Companionship: The Future of Feminist Biblical Studies and Feminism', in A. Brenner and C. Fontaine (eds), *A Feminist Companion to Reading the Bible: Approaches, Methods and Strategies*, Sheffield: Sheffield Academic Press: 39–60.

Morgan, R. and Barton, J. (1988), *Biblical Interpretation*, Oxford: Oxford University Press.

Mosala, I. J. (1993), 'Biblical Hermeneutics and Black Theology in South Africa', in N. K. Gottwald and R. A. Horsley (eds), *The Bible and Liberation: Political and Social Hermeneutics*, Maryknoll, NY: Orbis Books: 51–73.

Moulton, R. J. (1900), *A Short Introduction to the Literature of the Bible*, London: D.C. Heath and Co.

Moxnes, H. (2001), 'The Construction of Galilee as a Place for the Historical Jesus – Part I', *BTB* 31: 26–37 (Part II, 64–77).

Muilenburg, J. (1956), 'Introduction and Exegesis to Isaiah, Chapters 40–66', in G. A. Buttrick (ed.), *The Interpreter's Bible*, vol. 5, Nashville: Abingdon-Cokesbury: 381–773.

— (1969), 'Form Criticism and Beyond', *JBL* 88: 1–18 (repr. in P. R. House [ed.], *Beyond Form Criticism: Essays in Old Testament Literary Criticis*m, Winona Lake, Indiana: Eisenbrauns, 1992: 49–69).

Nadar, S. (2006), '"*Barak* God and Die!": Women, HIV, and a Theology of Suffering', in R. S. Sugirtharajah (ed.), *Voices from the Margin: Interpreting the Bible in the Third World*, Maryknoll, NY: Orbis Books: 189–203.

Newsom, C. A. and Ringe, S. H. (eds) (1992), *The Women's Bible Commentary*, London: SPCK; Louisville, KY: Westminster John Knox Press.

Nissinen, M. (2009), 'Reflections on the "Historical-Critical" Method: Historical Criticism and Critical Historicism', in J. M. LeMon and K. H. Richards (eds), *Method Matters: Essays on the Interpretation of the Hebrew Bible in Honor of David L. Petersen*, Atlanta, GA: Society of Biblical Literature: 479–504.

Osiek, C. (1985), 'The Feminist and the Bible: Hermeneutical Alternatives', in A. Y. Collins (ed.), *Feminist Perspectives on Biblical Scholarship*, Atlanta, GA: Scholars Press: 93–105.

Pardes, I. (1992), *Countertraditions in the Bible: A Feminist Approach*, Cambridge, MA and London: Harvard University Press.

Patrick, D., and Scult, A. (eds) (1990), *Rhetoric and Biblical Interpretation*, Sheffield: Almond Press.

Pippin, T. (1996), 'Ideology, Ideological Criticism, and the Bible', *Currents in Research: Biblical Studies* 4: 51–78.

Porter, S. E. and Stamps, D. L. (eds) (2002), *Rhetorical Criticism of the Bible*, Sheffield: Sheffield Academic Press.

Postmodern Bible: The Bible and Culture Collective (1995), New Haven and London: Yale University Press.

Powell, M. A. (2011), *Chasing the Eastern Star: Adventures in Biblical Reader-Response Criticism*, Louisville, KY: Westminster John Knox Press.

Prior, M. (1997), *The Bible and Colonialism: A Moral Critique*, Sheffield: Sheffield Academic Press.

Provan, I. W. (1995), 'Ideologies, Literary and Critical: Reflections on Recent Writing on the History of Israel', *JBL* 114: 585–606.

Pui-lan, K. (2005), *Postcolonial Imagination and Feminist Theology*, Louisville, KY: Westminster John Knox Press.

Quint, D. (1993), *Epic and Empire: Politics and Generic Form from Virgil to Milton*, Princeton, NJ: Princeton University Press.

Rad, G. von (1965), 'The Beginnings of Historical Writing in Ancient Israel', in G. von Rad, *The Problem of the Hexateuch and Other Essays*, Edinburgh: Oliver and Boyd: 166–204.

— (1972; rev. edn), *Genesis: A Commentary*, London: SCM Press; Philadelphia: Westminster Press.

Ramsey, G. W. (1981), *The Quest for the Historical Israel: Reconstructing Israel's Early History*, London: SCM Press.

Reif, S. (1998), 'Aspects of the Jewish Contribution to Biblical
 Interpretation', in J. Barton (ed.), *The Cambridge Companion to
 Biblical Interpretation*, Cambridge: Cambridge University Press:
 143–59.

Renan, E. (1927), *The Life of Jesus*, New York: Modern Library (trans.
 Charles E. Wilbour of *La Vie de Jésus*, Paris: Michel Lévy Frères, 1863).

Ruether, R. R. (ed.) (1974), *Religion and Sexism: Images of Woman in
 the Jewish and Christian Traditions*, New York: Simon and Schuster.

— (1982), 'Feminism and Patriarchal Religion: Principles of Ideological
 Critique of the Bible', *JSOT* 22: 54–66.

— (1985), 'Feminist Interpretation: A Method of Correlation', in L.
 M. Russell (ed.), *Feminist Interpretation of the Bible*, Philadelphia:
 Westminster Press: 111–124.

Russell, L. M. (1985a), 'Authority and the Challenge of Feminist
 Interpretation', in L. M. Russell (ed.), *Feminist Interpretation of the
 Bible*, Philadelphia: Westminster Press: 137–46.

— (1985b), *Feminist Interpretation of the Bible*, Philadelphia:
 Westminster Press.

Said, E. W. (1978), *Orientalism*, London: Routledge and Kegan Paul.

Schökel, L. Alonso (1998), *A Manual of Hermeneutics* (*The Biblical
 Seminar* 54), Sheffield: Sheffield Academic Press.

Schottroff, L., Schroer, S. and Wacker, M.-T. (eds) (1998), *Feminist
 Interpretation: The Bible in Women's Perspective* (trans.
 M. Rumscheidt and B. Rumscheidt), Minneapolis: Fortress Press.

Schüssler Fiorenza, E. (1982), 'Feminist Theology and New Testament
 Interpretation', *JSOT* 22: 32–46.

— (1983), *In Memory of Her: A Feminist Theological Reconstruction of
 Christian Origins*, New York: Crossroad Publishing Company.

— (1984), *Bread Not Stone: The Challenge of Feminist Biblical
 Interpretation*, Edinburgh: T & T Clark; Boston: Beacon Press.

— (1985a), 'Remembering the Past in Creating the Future: Historical–
 Critical Scholarship and Feminist Biblical Interpretation', in A. Y.
 Collins (ed.), *Feminist Perspectives on Biblical Scholarship*, Atlanta,
 GA: Scholars Press: 43–63.

— (1985b), 'The Will to Choose or to Reject: Continuing our Critical
 Work', in L. M. Russell (ed.), *Feminist Interpretation of the Bible*,
 Philadelphia: Westminster Press: 125–36.

— (1993), 'Transforming the Legacy of *The Woman's Bible*', in
 E. Schüssler Fiorenza (ed.), *Searching the Scriptures, Volume One: A
 Feminist Introduction*, London: SCM Press; New York: Crossroad
 Publishing Company: 1–24.

— (1998), *Sharing her Word: Feminist Biblical Interpretation in
 Context*, Boston: Beacon Press.

— (1999), *Rhetoric and Ethic: The Politics of Biblical Studies*, Minneapolis: Fortress Press.

Schwartz, R. M. (ed.) (1990), *The Book and the Text: The Bible and Literary Theory*, Oxford: Basil Blackwell.

Setel, T. D. (1985), 'Prophets and Pornography: Female Sexual Imagery in Hosea', in L. M. Russell (ed.), *Feminist Interpretation of the Bible*, Philadelphia: Westminster Press: 86–95.

Shanks, H. (ed.) (1995), *Feminist Approaches to the Bible*, Washington, DC: Biblical Archaeological Society.

Skinner, J. (1930; rev. edn), *A Critical and Exegetical Commentary on Genesis*, Edinburgh: T & T Clark.

Soares-Prabhu, G. M. (2006), 'Two Mission Commands: An Interpretation of Matthew 28: 16–20 in the Light of a Buddhist Text', in R. S. Sugirtharajah (ed.), *Voices from the Margin: Interpreting the Bible in the Third World*, Maryknoll, NY: Orbis Books: 331–46.

Spencer, R. A. (1980), *Orientation by Disorientation: Studies in Literary Criticism and Biblical Literary Criticism Presented in Honor of William A. Beardslee*, Pittsburgh: Pickwick.

Stanton, E. Cady (ed.) (Part I, 1895; Part II, 1898), *The Woman's Bible*, Edinburgh: Polygon Books; New York: European Publishing Company (reprinted New York: Arno Press, 1974).

Sternberg, M. (1985), *The Poetics of Biblical Narrative: Ideological Literature and the Drama of Reading*, Bloomington, IN: Indiana University Press.

Strauss, D. F. (1879), *A New Life of Jesus*, London: Williams and Norgate (trans. *Das Leben Jesu*, published in 1835).

Sugirtharajah, R. S. (1998), 'A Postcolonial Exploration of Collusion and Construction in Biblical Interpretation', in R. S. Sugirtharajah (ed.), *The Postcolonial Bible*, Sheffield: Sheffield Academic Press: 91–116.

— (2001), *The Bible and the Third World: Precolonial, Colonial and Postcolonial Encounters*, Cambridge: Cambridge University Press.

— (2002), *Postcolonial Criticism and Biblical Interpretation*, Oxford: Oxford University Press.

— (2006), 'Postcolonial Biblical Interpretation', in R. S. Sugirtharajah (ed.), *Voices from the Margin: Interpreting the Bible in the Third World*, Maryknoll, NY: Orbis Books: 64–84.

Sugirtharajah, R. S. (ed.) (1998), *The Postcolonial Bible*, Sheffield: Sheffield Academic Press.

— (ed.) (1999), *Vernacular Hermeneutics*, Sheffield: Sheffield Academic Press.

— (ed.) (2006a; rev. edn), *Voices from the Margin: Interpreting the Bible in the Third World*, Maryknoll, NY: Orbis Books.

— (ed.) (2006b), *The Postcolonial Biblical Reader*, Oxford: Blackwell Publishing Ltd.

Suleiman, S. R. and Crosman, I. (eds) (1980), *The Reader in the Text. Essays on Audience and Interpretation*, Princeton: Princeton University Press.

Tannehill, R. C. (1977), 'The Disciples in Mark: The Function of a Narrative Role', *JR* 57: 386–405.

Thatcher, A. (2008), *The Savage Text: The Use and Abuse of the Bible*, Oxford: Wiley-Blackwell.

Thiselton, A. C. (1992), *New Horizons in Hermeneutics: The Theory and Practice of Transforming Biblical Reading*, Grand Rapids, MI: Zondervan Publishing House.

Thompson, T. L. (1992), *Early History of the Israelite People from the Written and Archaeological Sources*, Leiden: Brill.

Tollerton, D. (2007), 'Emancipation from the Whirlwind: Piety and Rebellion among Jewish-American Post-Holocaust and Christian Liberation Readings of Job', *Studies in Christian-Jewish Relations* 2: 70–91.

Tompkins, J. P. (ed.) (1980), *Reader-Response Criticism. From Formalism to Post-Structuralism*, Baltimore: The Johns Hopkins University Press.

Trible, Ph. (1978), *God and the Rhetoric of Sexuality*, London: SCM Press; Philadelphia: Fortress Press.

— (1985), 'Postscript: Jottings on the Journey', in L. M. Russell (ed.), *Feminist Interpretation of the Bible*, Philadelphia: Westminster Press: 147–9.

— (1989), 'Bringing Miriam out of the Shadows', *Bible Review* 5: 14–25.

— (1994), *Rhetorical Criticism: Context, Method and the Book of Jonah*, Minneapolis: Fortress Press.

— (1995), 'Eve and Miriam: From the Margins to the Center', in H. Shanks (ed.), *Feminist Approaches to the Bible*, Washington, DC: Biblical Archaeological Society: 5–24.

Tull, P. K. (1999), 'Rhetorical Criticism and Intertextuality', in S. L. McKenzie and S. R. Haynes (eds), *To Each its Own Meaning: An Introduction to Biblical Criticism and their Application*, Louisville, KY: Westminster John Knox Press: 156–80.

Vawter, B. (1977), *On Genesis: A New Reading*, London: Geoffrey Chapman.

Wacker, M.-T. (1998), 'Historical, Hermeneutical, and Methodological Foundations', in L. Schottroff, S. Schroer and M.-T. Wacker (eds), *Feminist Interpretation: The Bible in Women's Perspective* (trans. M. Rumscheidt and B. Rumscheidt), Minneapolis: Fortress Press: 3–82.

Walker, A. (1983), *In Search of our Mothers' Gardens: Womanist Prose*, New York: Harcourt, Brace and Jovanovich.

Warner, M. (ed.) (1990), *The Bible as Rhetoric: Studies in Biblical Persuasion and Credibility*, London: Routledge.

Warrior, R. A. (2006), 'A Native American Perspective: Canaanites, Cowboys and Indians', in R. S. Sugirtharajah (ed.), 2006a: 235–41.

Watson, D. F. and Hauser, A. J. (1994), *Rhetorical Criticism of the Bible: A Comprehensive Bibliography with Notes on History and Method*, Leiden: Brill.

Weems, R. J. (1993; rev. edn), 'Reading her Way through the Struggle: African American Women and the Bible', in N. K. Gottwald and R. A. Horsley (eds), *The Bible and Liberation: Political and Social Hermeneutics*, Maryknoll, NY: Orbis Books: 31–50.

— (2006), 'Re-reading for Liberation: African American Women and the Bible', in R. S. Sugirtharajah (ed.), *Voices from the Margin: Interpreting the Bible in the Third World*, Maryknoll, NY: Orbis Books: 27–39.

Wellek, R. and Warren, A. (1984; 3rd edn), *Theory of Literature*, New York and London: Harcourt Brace and Company.

West, G. O. (1993), *Contextual Bible Study*, Pietermaritzburg: Cluster Publications.

— (1995; 2nd rev. edn), *Biblical Hermeneutics of Liberation: Modes of Reading the Bible in the South African Context*, Pietermaritzburg: Cluster Publications; Maryknoll, NY: Orbis Books.

— (1999), *The Academy of the Poor: Towards a Dialogical Reading of the Bible*, Sheffield: Sheffield Academic Press.

West G. O. with Musa W. Dube (ed.) (1996), *"Reading With": An Exploration of the Interface between Critical and Ordinary Readings of the Bible* (*Semeia* 75), Atlanta, GA: Scholars Press.

Whitelam, K. W. (1984), 'The Defence of David', *JSOT* 29: 61–78.

— (1986), 'Recreating the History of Israel', *JSOT* 35: 45–70.

— (1989), 'Israelite Kingship. The Royal Ideology and its Opponents', in R. E. Clements (ed.), *The World of Ancient Israel: Sociological, Anthropological and Political Perspectives*, Cambridge: Cambridge University Press: 119–39.

Willard, F. E. (1889), *Woman in the Pulpit*, Chicago: Woman's Temperance Publication Association.

Wimsatt, W. K. and Beardsley, M. (1946) 'The Intentional Fallacy', *Sewanee Review* 54 (reprinted in W. K. Wimsatt, *The Verbal Icon:*

Studies in the Meaning of Poetry, London: Methuen and Company Ltd: 1970: 3–18).

Wink, W. (1973), *The Bible in Human Transformation*, Philadelphia: Fortress Press.

Winterowd, W. R. (1968), *Rhetoric: A Synthesis*, New York: Holt, Rinehart & Winston.

Wuellner, W. (1987), 'Where is Rhetorical Criticism Taking us?' *CBQ* 49: 448–63.

INDEX OF BIBLICAL REFERENCES

INDEX OF SUBJECTS

INDEX OF MODERN AUTHORS